VAGABONDING

VAGABONDING

In Defense and Praise of Millennial Faith

Laurie Lyter Bright

CASCADE *Books* • Eugene, Oregon

VAGABONDING
In Defense and Praise of Millennial Faith

Copyright © 2018 Laurie Lyter Bright. All rights reserved. Except for brief quotations in critical publications or reviews, no part of this book may be reproduced in any manner without prior written permission from the publisher. Write: Permissions, Wipf and Stock Publishers, 199 W. 8th Ave., Suite 3, Eugene, OR 97401.

Cascade Books
An Imprint of Wipf and Stock Publishers
199 W. 8th Ave., Suite 3
Eugene, OR 97401

www.wipfandstock.com

PAPERBACK ISBN: 978-1-5326-1918-2
HARDCOVER ISBN: 978-1-4982-4535-7
EBOOK ISBN: 978-1-4982-4534-0

Cataloguing-in-Publication data:

Names: Bright, Laurie Lyter, author.
Title: Vagabonding : in defense and praise of millennial faith / Laurie Lyter Bright.
Description: Eugene, OR : Cascade Books, 2018.
Identifiers: ISBN 978-1-5326-1918-2 (paperback) | ISBN 978-1-4982-4535-7 (hardcover) | ISBN 978-1-4982-4534-0 (ebook)
Subjects: LCSH: Generation Y—Religious life.
Classification: BV4529.2 B74 2018 (print) | BV4529.2 B74 (ebook)

Manufactured in the USA.   NOVEMBER 28, 2018

Scripture quotations are from:

New Revised Standard Version Bible, copyright © 1989 National Council of the Churches of Christ in the United States of America. Used by permission. All rights reserved.

And THE HOLY BIBLE, NEW INTERNATIONAL VERSION® NIV® Copyright © 1973, 1978, 1984 by International Bible Society® Used by permission. All rights reserved worldwide.

Dedication

I am now and always grateful for my sister, Becky McCleery, for helping me see past my doubts and inspiring me to do better for the world.

For my mom, who taught me my voice mattered (among many other things), and for my dad, who was the first person to suggest I had a voice others might want to read (but not without some serious red-pen editing first!).

For Natalie, Carter, and Lily: keep shining, you beautiful, inspiring ones. Watching you become yourselves is the joy of this aunt's life.

For my grandma, who at ninety exemplifies a willingness to balance the world as it is and an unimaginably strong faith with a sense of humor about it all. Grandma, you're who I hope I become.

For Jesse: all that I have and all that I am, I give to you.

And for Baby Girl Bright on her way: Welcome to the world, little one. Now go let's change it.

Table of Contents

Acknowledgments ix

Introduction – A Word on Privilege, Context, and Perspective xi

1 Mary, Martha, and New Hospitality
   (Or High Noon over Tablecloths) 1

2 Why We Don't Do Committees 12

3 Judas Iscariot the Irreplaceable
   and the Radical Othering of Self 29

4 Thomas and Un-curated Faith in the Snapchat Generation 36

5 The Great Commission and the Global Generation 44

6 Family of Choice 55

7 Ancient Made New: Unbounded Love and Globalism 62

8 Instagram Faith: Crucifixion Instantaneous 73

9 Beloved Disciples and Authenticity of Faith 85

10 Passion under Pressure 95

11 Can't Buy This Love: Offering and Millennial Faith 106

12 The Revolution will be Tweeted 115

Conclusion 123

Acknowledgments

This book would have been impossible without the practical, tangible help of the crowd of ludicrous and lovely people who make my life complete. The stories and ideas herein are my own, and the stories are an amalgamation of characters and experiences rather than descriptions of one specific person or place. No one's ideas are entirely her own, however, and all I write comes from the lives entwined in mine. There are many people to thank.

For Taylor Brown for her editorial talents and strange hybrid knowledge of theology and youth culture on social media. For Angela Cummins for literally giving me a place to write. For the many others who listened, critiqued, and supported along the way. Miss Halvorson and Mrs. Steele (because a promise is a promise), and Revs. Drs. Kathy and Greg Bostrom and Rev. Gregg Dana for mentoring me all along. For the good people at Wildwood Presbyterian Church who raised me up in love, baptized, confirmed, and ordained me, and let me be a pain in the church's collective neck. For the kind and brave people of First United Presbyterian Church in Loveland, Colorado, who took a first chance on me as their pastor and loved me with all my flaws, my profound gratitude.

INTRODUCTION

A Word on Privilege, Context, and Perspective

A Love Letter

Dear Church,

Church as I know you, and church as you've been, and church as you might yet be: I am with you. Every book comes from a perspective and this is mine: I was born and raised in the Presbyterian Church (USA). I was baptized, confirmed, and ordained in the same church that confirmed my dad, the same church my family—from cousins to grandma—attend, and the church where I learned to be Christian under the guidance of numerous Sunday school teachers, faith partners, and musicians. I grew up with a wife-and-husband preacher team and did not think for one second it would be strange for a woman to preach. I was encouraged, loved, and supported in understanding how the church worked, encouraged through the sometimes grueling and often ridiculous ordination process of the PC (USA), and weekly church attendance was part of my normal.

So church, I love you. I think you do a lot that's amazing.

I also think you, we, all of us need some firm nudging along the path and I have witnessed enough churches getting stuck to consider it worth throwing in my two cents about how we unstick.

For some reason, we are all stuck on millennials. There are about 73 million of us in the US. In article after article, the collective worry deepens regarding what exactly millennials are doing to destroy the world as we

A Word on Privilege, Context, and Perspective

know it. In this way, fear is rallied, and it is unaccompanied by understanding. It's dangerous to treat any group as a monolith and millennials are no exception. Of course, this is a diverse group of beliefs and practices. We populate all aspects of the sociopolitical spectrum and the geographic possibilities, and hold dear any number of worldviews and values.

I am writing, therefore, not to convince you that all millennials are anything, but to help you (the church) get excited about us! We come not just with spotty attendance and a confusing concept of giving, but with ideas, life experiences, and passionate commitment. We have a lot to offer the church. You just have to let us in—really in—to your hearts as much as to your fellowship halls.

I say "us" because I am also, technically, a millennial. Right on the common line used to differentiate Generation X and millennials, I feel too old to relate to much of youth culture; I write this at age 33—what I playfully term my Jesus year which is, by the way, an excellent way to torpedo a date that's going poorly. "So . . . you're in your Jesus year, huh?" "My what?" "Your Jesus year. You know, the age Jesus was when he died." "Oh." "Yeah . . . so . . . How's that going? Feeling sufficiently accomplished yet?" (I've used this method to end dates. It works. It's okay, I met someone who I didn't have to torpedo.) Yet my birth year is what it is, so a millennial I suppose I am.

Being a millennial means I grew up without a cell phone, had my first foray into the world of AIM chatting in early high school, and turned in most of my college assignments by hand rather than online. It also means I was among the first wave of Facebookers when Facebook was introduced to the college scene and joined my peers in early adoption of texting as a preferred mode of communication. I'll confess to minimal personal commitment to social media, not having bothered to keep up with personal use of Twitter, Instagram, Snapchat, etc., except as concerns the times I've served in youth ministry. I'm no Luddite, I just didn't keep up with it.

I grew up with friends of various races, faith systems, and gender identities, and the gay/straight alliance at my high school struck me as an obvious manifestation of that whole "love thy neighbor" thing.

Some basic constructs to define: a millennial does have some actual borders. Loosely defined as someone who reaches young adulthood in the early part of the twenty-first century, the birth years of millennials run from approximately 1980 to the late 1990s. Millennialism is largely a Western construct, and general conceptions of millennial identity hinge on

A Word on Privilege, Context, and Perspective

growing up in societies that are capitalist, representatively governed, and US-European focused, though certainly millennial identities manifest on a global scale.

Beyond my spot in the millennial crowd, my own biases lace my window into this world: I'm a cisgender, white, middle-class, heterosexual, married female in the US and I can speak for no one but myself. I look forward to hearing more voices from millennials of other faiths, families, cultures, and contexts on their own experiences and worldviews. None of us are any one thing.

And the church—there is no one simple definition there either. She is a somewhat ornery, extraordinary creature, not unlike most of those who populate her pews. In the US, she is too often co-opted for political gain. She is used to preach exclusion and veil hate. She is also resilient beyond belief, remaining tender in the tumult, persisting with loving communities, quilting groups and choir robes, Sunday schools and car wash fundraisers. The love ethic at the heart of the teachings of Jesus Christ manages to persist through us and in spite of us.

Finally, this book is not intended to apply to every context any more than every millennial. In the pages that follow, you'll find a mix of the sacred and ordinary, the silly and sublime, as we consider various figures of early church life in light of the millennial generation. It is a project based in playfulness, meant to cajole us (all of us) out of the fearful dark and into one possible future; one in which we can see each other more clearly.

I come to you not with a sword, but an offering: consider thinking about the upcoming generations in a new way. Leave room for the possibility that millennials have more to offer than a potential boost to attendance and offering. Leave room for new conversations. Leave room for all we might learn from each other.

Let's stay open and see what God does in the mix.

With love,

Laurie

CHAPTER 1

Mary, Martha, and New Hospitality

(Or High Noon over Tablecloths)

Luke 10:38-42 (NRSV)

Jesus Visits Martha and Mary

> 38*Now as they went on their way, he entered a certain village, where a woman named Martha welcomed him into her home.* 39*She had a sister named Mary, who sat at the Lord's feet and listened to what he was saying.* 40*But Martha was distracted by her many tasks; so she came to him and asked, "Lord, do you not care that my sister has left me to do all the work by myself? Tell her then to help me."* 41*But the Lord answered her, "Martha, Martha, you are worried and distracted by many things;* 42*there is need of only one thing. Mary has chosen the better part, which will not be taken away from her."*

It was about 8 a.m., but, in sharper reality, it was high noon in the fellowship hall. Sunday. The calm before the storm. Danger was in the air. Danger, and the musty smell of slightly stale coffee, heavy as the aging building and its accompanying sweltering heat from an overactive boiler. The room itself seemed to sweat, drops of perspiration gathered above the pursed lips of the disapproving women at the center of this space. These women, members and the heartbeat of this small church community, muttered audibly, arms crossed, in clear disgust as they contemplated the pre-coffee-hour catastrophe.

Someone had taken home the tablecloths—those white linen catch-alls of crumbs that held the church's tableau of fellowship together, those crumbs that would be blamed on children and coffee spills in the shaky hands of the church elders. The tablecloths were the symbol of purity and beauty, ready to catch the small talk and foster the connections of a time of fellowship. These tablecloths, normally tended to by the self-appointed kitchen czars and caretakers of the church, were not in order. *Someone* had washed them. *Someone* had returned them. And *someone* had committed the gravest of sins—a failure to iron.

Why would someone bother to take them home and return them like this?

That is just the laziest damn thing.

Look at this! We can't set them out like this.

I'll have to do it over—if you want it done right, you have to do it yourself.

In a breath, the tables were swept clear of their somewhat wrinkled cloths and bundled into the backseat of the car of a more attentive laundress. Silk flower arrangements were lightly dusted off and placed on a doily at the center of each scratched, bare, brown table. A final glance around the room and a sigh of mild disgust, and the pronouncement was made—*I guess that's as good as it's going to get this week.* As I readied myself to enter the pulpit, I muttered too—my consistent prayer before leading worship: *God, keep me out of Your way.* About the great tablecloth debacle, however, I never said a word.

This high-noon moment of indirect accusations and obvious distress illuminated a level of betrayal of church norms that I would not have imagined possible. This was not a failure to iron. This was a transgression. This was a showdown between a generational Mary and generational Marthas.

Confession to the reader: that *someone* was me. As a twenty-eight-year-old, single female solo pastor living far from family and friends, the role of minister was a minefield of such scenarios. My utterly non-domestic self, attempting to make good on the expectations of my gender, age, or role, helping to maintain order and upkeep when possible, but as discreetly as possible to avoid trapping my role with future expectations. The tablecloths were gross the previous week, and I didn't want to presume a parishioner would do a task I was unwilling to do myself. So I washed them. I dried them. And I failed to iron them.

I've spent an inordinate amount of time considering why I didn't iron those tablecloths, or more to the point, why I didn't fess up to the fact that I was the non-ironing villain. This wasn't just about gender roles, though in all the muttering I never once heard it considered that a man had done the laundry. This wasn't just about territorialism, though that can be a huge issue in the microcosm of the church. This was generational. I didn't want them to see me and my cohort of millennials as lazy. I didn't want to admit to a failure in the eyes of women I loved and respected, nor feed assumptions about the newest generation of fully-fledged adults—that we are self-obsessed, ill-mannered, and indolent. Any millennial might be any or all of those things, but I didn't want to add to the charge. And, perhaps most precisely, I didn't understand why this was such a big deal. The tablecloths looked fine to me and would undoubtedly be covered in crumbs and spills again momentarily, and I really couldn't comprehend using white tablecloths at all since people are inherently messy creatures. But I knew I had broken some sacred code of respect between my elders and me. I had entered their world of hospitality and disregarded the rules in favor of my own sense of what made a welcoming community. I was the irresponsible sister.

Hospitality Renaissance

This tablecloth breach is, of course, symbolic. The church the boomers have built is one of traditional hospitality. Hospitality in the form of potlucks (or pitch-ins, depending on your geography), spaghetti dinner fundraisers, ladies' teas, and sewing circles. Hospitality that presents a thoughtful and beloved institution—we do this every year, and it is who we are. Come join us for the rummage sale! You are welcome to come to our dinners and seniors' outings. You should bring your friend to our Christmas pageant and we always buy lilies at Easter. This is our church, and we would love for you to be a part of it.

This is the hospitality of Martha welcoming Christ into her home, and it is as true an expression of love now as it was for dear Martha. Martha, whom Jesus calls by name and clearly loves. She approaches him with directness and familiarity, asking whether or not he sees and recognizes her work and her sister's shirking of her responsibility. Imploring him to get her the help she needs to keep things moving. She wants to be noticed and, in order to feel validated, Martha needs her work to be seen. Christ sees her desire to cultivate and prepare as the offering of her apron-wearing, hard-working heart. Just the same, our churches—scrubbed and created by the boomer generation—speak to a profound kind of love. This work speaks to a sense of calling to build a safe, orchestrated space. It ensures the place is clean and usable, the messes are cleaned, and there are no distractions on Sunday morning. Everything and everyone has their place in such a structure as this, and we would be happy to connect you with a greeter to show you where you might fit in too. The church of a Martha welcomes people in.

It is a misinterpretation to say Christ rebukes Martha in the aforementioned passage. He doesn't. Martha's *diakonia*, or tasks, are more akin to the kind of caring hospitality associated with service as a deacon than household cleaning. I like to think Christ sees the good in this, if not the primacy of it. What Martha is doing is not inherently bad or shameful, and Christ does not condemn or shame her. He sees her and he acknowledges her. He just doesn't let her take away Mary's devoted happiness in the process.

Instead of a reprimand, Christ sets up a dichotomy between need and distraction. It is not a condemnation of the activities that might be very good and valuable to do. It is simply a shift in focus, highlighting that there is really only one thing that is at the heart of faith, and that is attending foremost to Christ's presence, modeled here by Mary's rapt attention.

Often, the church of generations past has been most concerned with her own survival, and all maintenance serves that survival as a primary goal. How will we fill the pews? How many new members can we add? Will the budget cover new computers for the technology rotation of Sunday school? Who needs to be thanked at the Christian education breakfast? This is the busyness of church life, and in it many of us find meaning and connection. There are jobs to be done and, when they are executed flawlessly, the church appears healthy and thriving. There is nothing bad about wanting your church to be clean, welcoming, and orderly. I do not believe that such hospitality is dying. Rather, it is finding a new way to live.

Just as the Renaissance of fourteenth-century Europe did not signify the conclusion of all previous thinking, but rather embraced a new expression of beauty, so too does this renaissance of the hospitable church build upon what has come before. There is no Shakespeare without Ovid and Plutarch. Fear not—millennials arrive not to destroy your tablecloths, but rather to help build a new table.

Mary, Martha, and New Hospitality

Reframing Hospitality as an Act of Resistance

The church of Mary and the faith of millennials send people out. Millennials exist in a world that is inherently disordered, and it isn't any wonder that their church would reside in a little chaos. The average millennial will move and change careers more times than any generation before us. We are not rooted to any one place or identity, largely because we can't be. We move often and yet maintain the same desire to connect and love deeply as our predecessors. We know the urgency of forging those connections with beloved friends since, before long, they or we will move on once again.

And so we resist meetings and newsletters and anything that does not bring with it a sense of urgency. We may desire a physical space we can call church, but we more immediately crave people who connect with us like family. Research indicating a devaluing of institutional church affiliation amongst mainline millennials is missing the point. Such expressions are not necessarily a disavowal of the underlying spirit of the church, but a disavowal of the confines of the institution itself, predicated on welcoming us only on terms that fail to incorporate the lived realities of our generation. We do not desire an institution that only welcomes on decades-old and less-than-progressive terms.

Hospitality in the institutional church, and the boomer generation specifically, is a slow build toward connection. Attend a new-member class. Volunteer at a special service. Join a committee. Keep the tablecloths in pristine condition. Be reliable, patient, humble, and steadfast. Faith is built on the foundation of presence, and that has worked historically because that presence was reliable. It was less common for an individual or family to arrive, join a community of faith, and leave again within a few years. People built lives on locations that were considered permanent. Your church was the church that baptized your babies, officiated their weddings, and would eventually bury you. Your church was housed in a brick building on a familiar corner, and there your church would remain for generations to come. Practices of welcoming center on the preservation of the institution and the inclusion of outsiders in it.

The church of the millennial centers around hospitality of the person, identifying the individual and cultural context and meeting where life happens, regardless of the institution. It cannot be programmed, mandated, or mildly tweaked by a committee with each new year. This is hospitality in consideration of the consistent rates of delayed marriage and having children, the dwindling likelihood of home ownership, and the strong possibility of geographic mobility in the millennial generation. The nature of this world requires hospitality that meets people where they are and where they may be headed. This hospitality of the person is borne of necessity, not merely obstinacy. We don't place the same value on decorations, or even on physical spaces, because physical space is impermanent to us. Where church (and the accompanying physical traditions of church) was once the space of safety, the fluidity of the millennial generation requires a more expansive view of sanctuary. It is not physical. It is personal, because it has to be. We do not rely on physical spaces to keep us connected or safe. We rely on people.

Hospitality in the millennial age is intimacy at break-neck speed. Knowing well that they may leave for a job or a relationship at any time at all, their engagement cannot be predicated or judged on the same values as generations past. Instead, they require a new set of parameters based on depth of relationship, honesty in spiritual journeying, and a willingness to be vulnerable for the sake of one another. Their presence cannot be relied upon, but this is not the death of the church. It may be the church's next great revival.

It is this intense seeking of a faith family that makes young millennial Christians such a handful for many of their predecessors and, simultaneously, such close kin to the early church. It is here that millennials so closely resemble Mary, kneeling at Christ's feet and disregarding the call to do the dishes because she needs something intangible and immediate.

The brothers and sisters of the early church were disciples who knew well the urgency of dismantling empire. As Christ so commanded, they spread the message of their beloved teacher far and wide, knowing that to do so was to directly encounter the empire that had crucified Christ. Their faith in the meaning behind the resurrection and their relationship as a community was what carried their faith forward, compelling them to seek new communities with whom to share the journey. They were hunted, and their sustenance and survival depended on finding one another in the darkness. They operated on an urgency that reflected apocalyptic theology and confidence in Christ's return as imminent. It is only logical that they would resist empire with all they had and seek the light. This is an ancient and yet new way of engaging with a community of faith.

Furthermore, the early church disciples and millennials share a sense of urgency around engaging a socially-diverse landscape. The early disciples did so out of necessity as a minority group in an empire-controlled place and time, a culture of insurgency and radicalized faith, and a world where there were dramatic ramifications for behavior deemed out of society's accepted social structures. This was their immediate world. In 2018, the entire world is immediate to millennials. This intensifies the desire to understand, connect, and express across bounds of race, gender identity, sexuality, religion, nation, or politics. Because the systemic nature of the world is so openly named and discussed today, millennials seek to build and carve welcome out of a frequently inhospitable world.

To take it one step further, the millennial appropriation of an evolving concept of hospitality is not only serving to resurrect an ancient practice, but acts as a site of resistance in a world of post-post-modernity. We are told our world is chaos, darkness, death, and destruction. We are given live feeds of beheadings, Facebook-public accounts of police shootings, and casualty counts on the deaths caused by drone strikes we help to fund. In all of this, we have a profound awareness that very few of us will ever have the security of home or career that our parents had. We will navigate the world we have inherited as a nomadic and unsettled generation. In such a world as this, so instantly and fully aware of the horrors of places like Syria or South Sudan, it is an act of great resistance for millennials to seek connection over self-promotion, authentic faith over rote ritual, and to attend with open ears rather than maintain what feels familiar. It is resistance declaring that what has worked for others and in other times will not work for us in this time and place, and we will therefore refuse replication and instead go out and seek. It disregards the welcome mat in favor of breaking bread in the homes of the newly and dearly beloved stranger.

Which returns us to the home of Martha and Mary, where Martha busies herself in the work of welcoming, and Mary attends like a thirsty woman brought to a well.

Christ's praise of Mary and gentle redirection of Martha is not meant to condemn the practices of those who have scrubbed a thousand dishes and arranged a thousand silk flowers near the pulpit for decades. It is meant to suggest this: that these women were sisters, and found a way to coexist in a house that welcomed Christ.

Sisters

By naming this distinction in a church of Mary and a church of Martha, we can begin to dismantle the notion that these two forces work in opposition to one another. Sure, Martha got annoyed with Mary for her apparent laziness. And Mary probably spent plenty of time rolling her eyes as Martha nagged her to pitch in. Meals, care, and compassion were all an expectation, and it was their role as women to do this work. And yet, in spite of all of their differences revealed in just two small passages of Scripture, these sisters remain in life together.

John 11:17–37 (NRSV)

17 When Jesus arrived, he found that Lazarus had already been in the tomb four days. 18 Now Bethany was near Jerusalem, some two miles away, 19 and many of the Jews had come to Martha and Mary to console them about their brother. 20 When Martha heard that Jesus was coming, she went and met him, while Mary stayed at home. 21 Martha said to Jesus, "Lord, if you had been here, my brother would not have died. 22 But even now I know that God will give you whatever you ask of him." 23 Jesus said to her, "Your brother will rise again." 24 Martha said to him, "I know that he will rise again in the resurrection on the last day." 25 Jesus said to her, "I am the resurrection and the life. Those who believe in me, even though they die, will live, 26 and everyone who lives and believes in me will never die. Do you believe this?" 27 She said to him, "Yes, Lord, I believe that you are the Messiah, the Son of God, the one coming into the world." 28 When she had said this, she went back and called her sister Mary, and told her privately, "The Teacher is here and is calling for you." 29 And when she heard it, she got up quickly and went to him. 30 Now Jesus had not yet come to the village, but was still at the place where Martha had met him. 31 The Jews who were with her in the house, consoling her, saw Mary get up quickly and go out. They followed her because they thought that she was going to the tomb to weep there. 32 When Mary came where Jesus was and saw him, she knelt at his feet and said to him, "Lord, if you had been here, my brother would not have died." 33 When Jesus saw her weeping, and the Jews who came with her also weeping, he was greatly disturbed in spirit and deeply moved. 34 He said, "Where have you laid him?" They said to him, "Lord, come and see." 35 Jesus began to weep. 36 So the Jews said, "See how he loved him!" 37 But some of them said, "Could not he who opened the eyes of the blind man have kept this man from dying?"

Martha and Mary level the same accusation at Christ: Lord, if you had been here, our brother would not have died. It is both an expression of absolute faith—a fervent belief that Christ could have saved him—and faith wrecked absolutely—the unasked question: so why didn't you? They speak from a place of identical hurt—their brother is dead and they believe Christ could have prevented it, and didn't. Martha runs ahead to meet Christ and lays down both her grief and faith. She speaks of her confidence in Christ, and yet her bewildering pain at the loss of her brother, and engages with Christ in a mindful way. He asks her what she believes and thinks, and she tells him, confirming her faith. His care for her is obvious by both his presence to console her and his willingness to engage with her. Yet Christ calls for Mary too, inexplicably wanting both sisters present, and it is upon seeing Mary's kneeling, abject faith, and sorrow that he becomes moved to action. He sees her weep and he weeps. He sees her passion and moves from passive to active. The time has arrived, it seems, for less talk and more action.

So too can it be in the church—that we remain in life together, with our hospitality, our love, our grief, and our passion woven together as an expression of faith. Here, both sisters exist to complete the narrative, grappling with shared grief, faith, and life. Both sisters come to Christ in the turmoil of faith and doubt, and Christ meets them there. Life in the church of millennials and boomers and every other generation can be much the same. We can meet each other in the common space with our uncommon experiences, and build hospitable space for all. To pull this off, though, we need to understand one another much, much better than we do.

Ask a New Question

It may seem that these two styles are diametrically opposed. These perspectives—that hospitality means to invite into set constructs or that hospitality means to step out into unknown spaces—are indeed a strong push-pull, and it would be easy for us to instead divide churches over it. We've done it for plenty of other reasons. We could design one church service or setting or style for the young and one for the older. We could tinker with staging and programming and other elements of design to try to entreat newcomers. We could even rely on strict tradition keeping—trusting that millennials will do as they wish with their inherited church when the previous generations have passed on. Or we could see this push-pull as a magnetic force that keeps the life of the church in perfect tension.

That tension allows us to resist frustration with the old unanswered questions and to create a new question altogether. Let's not ask: How do we engage millennials and make them feel welcome in our church? How do we get them to show up and commit and give and serve in our context? Instead, let's ask: How do millennials engage and express welcome? How did Mary show her love? And is that a part of who we are as a church?

This shift in the question opens wide the doors of opportunity. We don't need to figure out how to get millennials to conform to the traditions, nor do we need to disavow previous generations of their beloved practices. We need to collaborate and figure out how both ways of being can be expressions of the same church.

Let's consider what millennials do show up for, if not church. They show up in droves for community activism, for justice, for music, and for politics. They demonstrate again and again a desire to be in the public square, engaging in ideas that center around justice, a genuine act of faith if ever there was one. The millennial generation demonstrates a clear faith in the possible, alongside a dramatic knowledge of the nature of oppression and injustice. They show up to take apart systems, in part because they *believe* they can take apart systems. This generation tilts at windmills in a way the early disciples would understand.

In the culture of protests and music festivals, pub trivia and political rallies, the hospitality of millennials is evident. We want to see and we want to be seen, to know and be known.

Could, perhaps, the church exit its own doors and sense of self-preservation, and take to the streets to meet people where they are? Might the Lord's table exist outside the bounds of the church walls? If we built a sense of hospitality that was defined by where we go, how we connect, and whose voice we amplify, the institutional church might be pleasantly surprised by her sense of renewed energy and sense of place in society.

For established churches seeking to reimagine themselves in light of millennial values, the reflection must begin inside. How do we as a church family demand conformity and why? Do our processes honor journeys that look different from our own? Do we make it difficult for ourselves to meet people in an authentic, caring way? At every single committee meeting, the question must be asked: Does this exist to meet the world with Christ, or does this exist to preserve ourselves?

Hospitality in the hands of millennials may go through a healthy transition from welcoming in to encouraging out, back to the original nature of radical hospitality in discipleship. There may or may not be tablecloths in the years to come, but there will most certainly be an unimaginable amount of holy tables.

CHAPTER 2

Why We Don't Do Committees

John 1:35–42 (NRSV)

The First Disciples of Jesus

> 35 The next day John again was standing with two of his disciples, 36 and as he watched Jesus walk by, he exclaimed, "Look, here is the Lamb of God!" 37 The two disciples heard him say this, and they followed Jesus. 38 When Jesus turned and saw them following, he said to them, "What are you looking for?" They said to him, "Rabbi" (which translated means Teacher), "where are you staying?" 39 He said to them, "Come and see." They came and saw where he was staying, and they remained with him that day. It was about four o'clock in the afternoon. 40 One of the two who heard John speak and followed him was Andrew, Simon Peter's brother. 41 He first found his brother Simon and said to him, "We have found the Messiah" (which is translated Anointed). 42 He brought Simon to Jesus, who looked at him and said, "You are Simon son of John. You are to be called Cephas" (which is translated Peter).

Jesus is ace at the whole enigmatic thing. "Come and see." He so rarely answers a question straight on, but rather goes about it sideways, a sneaky invitation to the curiosity of his immediate disciples and all those who would follow.

In the ceaseless efforts of tilting at windmills (i.e. organizing a peaceful and functional body of humans), I fear we may have committed (not committed: committee-ed.) our way out of a "come and see" philosophy.

The enigmatic makes us nervous. It's human nature to be mildly distrustful of that which we don't know.

In a church I once served and love deeply, there was a gorgeous stained glass window. Actually, there were many gorgeous stained glass windows. In touring the numerous rooms and hidden closet spaces of this gigantic historical space with a self-appointed building steward, I discovered one in particular: a gorgeous, three-foot diameter rose window, covered in dust, and kept under lock and key—keys which remained with the one steward alone. I asked why this piece of sacred art was kept under lock and key, and was told that it was so the kids didn't get in there and wreck it. It had resided in this closet since it broke a few decades before, and neither the time nor resources had existed for restoration. My preaching wheels began to turn . . . Locked away for fear of what might happen, fear of breaking, the light never being allowed to shine through. The symbolism was irresistible.

I asked for the keys to the closet and I was met with a laugh and dismissal. When pushed on the grounds of my role as pastor, I was told "we'll just see about that, missy." (Yes, missy. At 5'2" and twenty-eight years old, I still had a long way to go toward earning the respect of the grumpy old church men department). Eventually the subject of the window would find its way to session minutes, motions to approve, artists' bids being reviewed, and eventually to a place on the wall, lit from within so the rich colors could be appreciated.

I presumed power but failed to understand the fear that lay beneath this protective stance. I wanted this man and this community to come and see from my perspective—that art was to be shared and celebrated, that hoarding our treasure was antithetical to the Christian life. But I failed to go and see from the opposing vantage point. I approached not with curiosity about why this protection and preservation meant so much, but with a determined need to uproot what I saw as a stagnant stance. I pushed a shift from an inner circle that existed long before me to one that more closely aligned with my priorities.

The Tiniest Kingdoms in All the Land

I'm not entirely sure why churches tend to pool around the tiniest fiefdoms of power that ever there were, but it seems to happen ubiquitously. It happens in big churches and little ones. It happens for pastors and members alike. It starts innocently enough: the people who gather around a project or priority bond over their shared work, those big thankless tasks of church life: organizing and labeling the kitchen once and for all, cleaning out the worship closet, organizing the volunteers for acolytes, deciding that "youth room" and "junk storage" occupying the same space is not sending the greatest message to our youth. The people gather and, in particular when we're Protestants, we know best how to bond over shared work. The work is done and the people are satisfied, declaring "It is good."

But then, somehow or other, the work becomes something bigger than the sum of its parts. The work becomes the thing to be protected. The notes in the kitchen ratchet up in their tone from "gentle reminder" to "veiled threats" to "open hostility." The youth are chastised when their room is less than pristine. Our need to control our work in its aftermath becomes the fiefdom of power and we will not let it go. I don't know why or how this happens as often and easily as it does, when people lose sight of relationships as the center of the church and become, instead, fixated on the work of maintaining it all, but it's a common symptom of church life.

On some level, I think we are aware we are polishing the ruins and rearranging deck chairs on the Titanic. Perhaps we are suffering under the collective delusion that any such group, so loosely comprised of anyone who walks in off the street, could ever survive for long. I am not pessimistic about the future of the church—far from it. I am, however, a realist that the church in her current incarnation is facing the painful phoenix fire regeneration that means we are going through massive changes, and that fear of change makes us humans act very strangely indeed. So we cling to what feels safe and we attempt to maintain things as they have been because that is our mooring in stormy seas.

Embracing safety as embodied in long-held traditions tends to feel foreign and frivolous to millennials, a generation convicted by values of progress, forward momentum, and creation of new ways of being. When change is the standard, self-imposed stagnancy doesn't make a great deal of sense. The church may then be at a crossroads when faced with whether to maintain herself, protecting the fiefdoms of her work, or crack open to the possibilities that lie ahead, untested, unknown, and in departure from the church as we know her.

Why We Don't Do Committees
Boardroom Culture in the Sanctuary

Matthew 4:18-22; 5:1-11 (NRSV)

Jesus Calls the First Disciples

¹⁸As he walked by the Sea of Galilee, he saw two brothers, Simon, who is called Peter, and Andrew his brother, casting a net into the sea—for they were fishermen. ¹⁹And he said to them, "Follow me, and I will make you fish for people." ²⁰Immediately they left their nets and followed him. ²¹As he went from there, he saw two other brothers, James son of Zebedee and his brother John, in the boat with their father Zebedee, mending their nets, and he called them. ²²Immediately they left the boat and their father, and followed him.

Once while Jesus was standing beside the lake of Gennesaret, and the crowd was pressing in on him to hear the word of God, ²he saw two boats there at the shore of the lake; the fishermen had gone out of them and were washing their nets. ³He got into one of the boats, the one belonging to Simon, and asked him to put out a little way from the shore. Then he sat down and taught the crowds from the boat. ⁴When he had finished speaking, he said to Simon, "Put out into the deep water and let down your nets for a catch." ⁵Simon answered, "Master, we have worked all night long but have caught nothing. Yet if you say so, I will let down the nets." ⁶When they had done this, they caught so many fish that their nets were beginning to break. ⁷So they signaled their partners in the other boat to come and help them. And they came and filled both boats, so that they began to sink. ⁸But when Simon Peter saw it, he fell down at Jesus' knees, saying, "Go away from me, Lord, for I am a sinful man!" ⁹For he and all who were with him were amazed at the catch of fish that they had taken; ¹⁰and so also were James and John, sons of Zebedee, who were partners with Simon. Then Jesus said to Simon, "Do not be afraid; from now on you will be catching people." ¹¹When they had brought their boats to shore, they left everything and followed him.

Peter, Andrew, James, and John are called into the life of discipleship. They do not church shop, sign in as visitors, respond to the welcome letter, fill out a new members interest card, followed by a three-part inquirers class, followed by a meeting with the ruling body of the church, followed by formal acceptance into the life of the church through ritual, liturgy, prayer, and song. They just ditch their fish and walk.

Yet these disciples also represent the epitome of the inner circle. Christ asks these seemingly ordinary men what they are seeking. And they respond simply through words and actions. They're looking for fish—food to eat, a catch to sell and sustain. They are searching for their livelihood. For a rabbi and the Messiah. For Jesus. These stories don't conflict—they simply say the same thing in different ways. They want to live. And Christ promises them life, which is enough for them to join in the central circle, the inner life of Christ's ministry.

Such informality might be anathema to much of the institutional church today—perhaps in part because it deprives us of the positivist quantifiable data that lets us know if we've met with any earthly success. How many new people joined this year? How shall we handle clearing the roles of those who haven't participated, pledged, or petitioned for the right to stay counted among us? Who will staff the Sunday school teaching rotation and how are we going to pull off the Christmas pageant? How will we know we succeed if no one is keeping track, or the numbers aren't growing, or the giving doesn't extend?

Success matters in our culture and to pretend we can keep that out of our churches is naïve. It folds in on us from all sides. Success screams at us from children's soccer games and emails marked urgent and everything, everything, everything demands urgent attention. The church being in the world and of the world was always going to be a part of this rushing, success-obsessed life. Our propensity toward building inner circles ensures our own board chairs and councils will strive toward these measures of success just the same.

The inner circle takes a variety of forms and functions depending on the lay leadership of your community. For the institutional church, the inner circle most closely resembles maintaining existing structures, with the boardroom culture a cross between *Mad Men* (though hopefully more sober and less misogynistic) and *The Office* (though hopefully more productive). We have our processes, our expectations of meetings' duration and distribution of work, and our beliefs about preparedness and progress locked in. One of the first moves a new PC (USA) pastor is encouraged to make is to read over all the old session meeting minutes because they are expected to reveal a great deal about the priorities of the community. I do not recommend attempting this for churches with more than 100 years of history. That said, the real point of interest in these minutes is not the recollection of which endeavors moved the congregation into action and which ones failed in committee, but the commitment to process that a community demonstrates. It allows us to look for what remains the same while the world around us has changed so dramatically. In many such settings, power structures remain hierarchical and the often-unnamed power of the pastor in charge usually moves the agenda along, often building it in the first place.

Power shakes out all kinds of ways in the life of the church. In the boomer model, adults—primarily those fifty and over—are the stewards of the community, and seek to find ways for younger people to plug into existing systems. If June is new to your community and your first response to her experience in education is that she would be perfect for teaching Sunday school, I'd wager that your inner circle is boomer-led. And you may be right—she might be amazing at Sunday school teaching, but treating people as plugs for the holes in existing programs rather than as sources of new, fresh light is a surefire way to prioritize system over person.

This can be remarkably comforting and at times necessary. Churches provide a sense of constancy in a community and having an idea of what to expect as a newcomer can feel immensely welcoming. Furthermore, practicing welcome is hard, especially for adults. Kids tend to just pick up and play, but the older we get, the harder it becomes to find where we fit in a new setting.

Embedded in the life of the institutional church is the sense that children and youth are important and are treated as consumers of church life. The role of women is often used to mark the relative progress and progressivism of a church, but I find the role of children and youth to be far more telling. If the structures—both physical and social—of the church are built to contain, quiet, and corral kids into behaviors and spaces deemed acceptable for them, then children are likely both beloved and thought of as consumers. They are welcome (at least in those specific spaces), but their value is little beyond cuteness and the vague optimism of having young people around. Do not mistake this for a call to the church to function as a site of entertainment for kids. I think there are enough competing efforts toward entertaining youth in the world, and what they need from the life of the church is quite the opposite of being mollified. Youth need and deserve to be treated as more than entertainment or those to be kept entertained, but instead as fully valued members of the community. The concept of treating youth and children as genuine knowledge-keepers and wise ones in the life of the church has gained traction in the past few decades. Still, it is desperately hard to make this value manifest in the life of the traditional church.

In Gen X, the first inheritors of the boomer, the Silent Generation, and the Greatest Generation church, the inner circle is now in their forties, making the significant shift from church receiver to church caregiver. As their own children begin to populate the life of the church, Generations X and Y hover in an in-between space, the extra-squeezed sandwich generation, typically having children later in life than generations before, having fewer children if and when they do, and needing to care for aging parents who are living significantly longer.

Many Gen Xers return to church in order for their children to experience a replication of their own childhood memories of church—when Sunday school and youth group were focal points of their social worlds. Such a return to a treasured safe space holds a mighty appeal in a world keen to make every potential danger felt with every click of the channel. When this return doesn't go as they remembered or hoped it might, the choice becomes whether to move on or stay and work to improve or restore the church, and this decision is a difficult one for busy parents hoping to keep their kids busy and safe. It could be argued that this represents our consumerist culture at work: that church is meant to provide for me and my family, give me what I want and need, and if it doesn't, I'm going to leave it or change it to make it fit. It could further be argued that this goes into simple nostalgia on the part of these Gen X and Yers, a yearning for a time that feels safer and simpler in their lives.

Simultaneously though, many Gen Xers have shifted away from formal faith practices outside of major holidays and milestones, which means that it's equally possible for a millennial seeking a place in the life of the church to come from an unchurched background as one steeped in theological tradition. The inner circle mutates as a result. We can no longer expect all those who attend a church to know the protocols of worship or respect the unwritten hierarchies of the church committee. We cannot hold quite so tightly to slotting visitors into preprogrammed places, trusting their knowledge of, and value in, such programs to be shared.

Or it could be that these in-between adults are tapping into a deep, humanity-wide need for soul and spiritual center. Seeking meaning, wisdom, and understanding, as well as seeking community around those shared pursuits, is a central facet to the human experience. Call it religion, spirituality, philosophy, whatever you like, there seems to be a nearly universal need to ground our life experiences. Common wisdom might suggest that we are moving further and further away from anything like a spiritual society, but that only stands true as long as we maintain a very narrow version of what it means to hold a spiritual center. The more expansive view of what that spiritual center could mean is one of the great gifts of the millennial generation.

According to a Pew Research Center Report in 2010, millennials are much more likely to self-profess as unaffiliated, atheist, agnostic, or "nothing in particular" than those generations before them, with 25 percent of us committing to our non-commitment as being unaffiliated with formal religious practices. That said, 68 percent still declared themselves as Christian by denomination, as opposed to 81 percent of older generations (Pew Forum on Research, 2010).

The reasons for this are everything from shifting values of social acceptance to different valuation of free time, and even to nonconforming work hours. The reasons aren't identical for any two millennials and excellent studies have been done to attempt to parse these generational shifts. What is more pertinent for the purposes of this book, however, are the statements about what these shifts mean and, specifically, what they say about millennials.

At this point we are all fairly weary of arguments that millennials are lazy, unfocused, and uncommitted to anything beyond themselves. I say "we" because I am betting non-millennials are weary of it too, yet the articles keep on coming. The belief persists that this generation is particularly entitled, self-absorbed, and unwilling to think of the greater good. These perceptions are just wrong.

What gets (mis)labeled as commitment phobia in millennials may sometimes be precisely that. We might be unwilling to commit to a weekly or monthly demand. We might be interested in prioritizing our freedom. Instead of dismissing it whole cloth, let's consider that it may instead be the kind of irritation with inauthentic existence in the institutional church that led the early disciples to leave behind their nets and follow him. Inauthenticity is a disintegrated life that keeps faith in the church-on-Sundays-box, distinct and discrete from the home box, the work box, the friendship box. Even within the church, we wage war with ourselves, compartmentalizing everything from flowers to faith formation in the name of efficiency and management at the expense of integrated lives.

Questioning the systems themselves, millennials are more inclined to poke the sleeping bear of tradition, including and especially in the church. Millennials tend to upset the balance with their requests to find a new table. Or living room. Or picnic blanket. Because maybe we feel out of place at your table. Maybe we want you to join us in constructing a new one.

The millennial generation also represents the most broadly inclusivity-minded generation the US has experienced. Uncritical participation in systems of power is no longer acceptable. We did not invent a critical paradigm or worldview—hardly—but we do inherit the generous fruits of that labor in learning to question systems all around us. In a generation of people steeped in civil rights, feminism, and active work in the realms of active anti-ableist, anti-racist, anti-transphobic, anti-Islamophobic action, millennials are quick to push back. Sometimes led by our elders, and sometimes led by ourselves, the international discourse pushes us further into progressive territory of interrogating just who we're okay with leaving out. And the answer, from a Christian perspective, ought to be: no one.

Radical inclusivity is a strong value among a generation raised to believe that everyone has a voice worth hearing and a story worth telling. We didn't have to grow up under government-enforced segregation, and many of us did grow up with women in positions of power around us, even and perhaps especially in the pulpit. The freedom to question was paid for by those who came before us, giving us expansive room to interrogate questions like Dr. Martin Luther King's concerning why Sunday at 11 a.m. remains the most segregated hour in our country, or why any qualified person of any orientation or identity should be denied a call to ordination. Note that I am not suggesting millennials are the only ones questioning these systems—that isn't the case at all. But the inner circle of our foremothers and forefathers in radically inclusive thought is being blown wide open. The interrogation of who we are and why is more acceptable than ever before.

And, for a generation breaking through the veneer of color blindness, we come prepared to recognize, honor, and appreciate difference. Many of us were raised with the pluralities of the eighties and nineties—that we're all God's children, deserving of love, and therefore can't we all just be kind to each other and get along. Not atrocious sentiments on their own, but the instantaneity of information on race-based violence and hatred in this nation has surely popped the illusion that we can afford to be indifferent to difference.

Instead, the millennial inner circle seeks to be more of an outer circle—a collection of all those on the margins and fringes, brought to a place of central value and respect, brought closer and clearer, eye-to-eye with those early disciples. Broad identification as misfits, nerds, fanatics of particular pop-cultural expressions, the millennial generation rallies behind and identifies as the freaks, geeks, outcasts, and outsiders. We take our fandoms seriously to an almost terrifying degree, and take pride in our status in cult followings. Even the sardonic philosophy most commonly ascribed to hipsters—that I only like bands you've never heard of—plays into this desire to be known as an aberration, unable to be pinned down by the mainstream. Because of our socioeconomic position, age, and interaction with technology, we revel in our misfitdom, since we are still unsure what the mainstream could hold for us.

I maintain hope in the delightful idea of the disciples being every bit the same misfits as we are. The disciples were a motley crew, in spite of the monochromatic and overly peaceful look Da Vinci gives us of the last supper. They were rife with mistrust, held a wide variety of life experiences, and held deep, often conflicting convictions and interpretations of Christ's will and words. Even before they become an established crew, there is little clear organization to determine how Christ selects his disciples. It seems to me that Christ saw more in them than we can see from the distance of 2,000 years, recognizing in each of them someone who was simultaneously of the world and on the fringes of it. Disliked for their occupations (tax collectors), or living somewhat isolated lives (fishermen), or simply men wandering with the crowd who we know very little about—each of them comes with their own baggage, even when Christ admonishes them to leave it all behind and follow him. They could not even fit in properly to the role of ragtag disciples, bickering among themselves over who knew best what was being asked of them and why. Yet follow they did, because each of them sought on some level that which Christ was offering: a depth of life they were seeking.

When it comes to it, I think many of us would answer in a similar fashion if Jesus met us the second we darkened the door of a church or temple or synagogue or mosque. What are you looking for? Life. We are looking for life. We might not be able to call it that for it hits a little too close to home and heart, but it is what persists underneath the surface. We can call it community or purpose or meaning, we can call it a faith family or a place for soul work and spiritual nourishment, a place to worship and serve, but in the end it all means the same thing: we are looking for life. Life full, deep, and rich, centering the meaningful and stepping away from all that serves to distract us from each other, from our souls, and from God.

Imagine if the expression that you were seeking authentic life was enough to get you welcomed right into the heartbeat of a faith community. Imagine if such an audacious claim was not simply considered weird and in poor taste. Consider how church might be if we were intentionally centered in seeking life together—not just rhetorically, but the blood and sinews of the church. Perhaps it is to such an authentic life that we are bound, or where we are going, or both.

Inner circles of the church are notoriously slow to change, marked by the bounds of memory, and eager for new membership that, if we're honest, does not proffer significant alterations to the status quo. The current (and recent) manifestations of inner circles do not exist to affect change. They function as a celebration of maintenance.

Regardless of denomination, leadership and lay leadership are rooted in historical tradition. We clergy are very bad at communicating the movement of spirit and understanding in the life of our denominations. I don't think most of us intend to hoard knowledge like treasure—most of us are just desperately trying to finish the newsletter on time (ahem . . . three days late), but the effect remains. We learn exciting things at conferences or through seminary friends and, if we move on that knowledge at all, it is to jump right into attempts at implementation. We pass along the news of big, interesting amendments at the denominational level.

Inner Circle of Denominational Gatherings: Fight Club, Clergy Edition

The first rule of clergy fight club is that we do not talk about clergy fight club. Seriously. We don't tell anybody back in the pews about it and we ensure that these gatherings are sufficiently boring and inconvenient that precisely no one's curiosity is piqued.

My experience is limited to the presbytery-level gatherings of the PC (USA). Our system of governance builds from the local (individual church sessions), to the semi-local (presbyteries, where geographically connected teaching elders or ministers and ruling elders or lay-leaders gather), to the somewhat bigger (synods), and up to the General Assembly. From that limited vantage point, it seems that denominational gatherings tend to be excellent microcosms from which to examine the generational divides. Though we are one body, we are coming at this church thing from vastly different angles.

There, I have seen the stalwarts of the church—the stewards of order, polity, and practice, keepers of institutional memory and the not-occasional grudge. They keep track of everyone, knowing who ought to be where, minding the minutes of every committee meeting, prepared with full reports to give and receive. For these participants, these gatherings encapsulate some piece of what it means to be the living and breathing church. They connect over casseroles in the dining area and argue staunchly over their votes and views. What happens in these spaces matters to the keepers of the denominational lifeblood.

There too, I have seen (and been) among the very young, referred to as "kiddo" and numerous variations thereupon, and in one horrifying instance "a sexy lady pastor" whose "bloomers were showing" (they were leggings. Opaque leggings. Under a dress. I digress.). I will own that I have gotten bored and zoned out in these meetings, as have many colleagues of my generational kin. Most of us are decently well-educated and widely read people, so I don't think a generic lack of attention span would cover the reasons why this might be. No, I think there is something deeper at work: a strong and clear sense that these places are not for us. I have seen my peers presumed ready to take on any of the inevitable technological crises in these meetings. I have sat in the back with those who, like me, could not take one more second of the endless recitation of busyness and business without attention to the slightest sense of urgency, except over decisions whose social moment have long since passed through the zeitgeist of wider culture. The inner circle of the denomination may be kind or welcoming, but it is not there for us.

While denominational gatherings are sometimes inspired by biblical tradition, more often than not, churches rest heavily on their own traditions. Whether started in the 1800s, or the 1980s, US churches live in their own pasts. There is no shame in loving your own history, and knowing from whence we came can help us chart a realistic path forward. Archivists, historians, and those with institutional memory are invaluable resources to any community. They can help access precedent and engage in the work of recognizing our own patterns—be they successful or self-defeating. We can't have a ready concept of where we're going without deep appreciation for where we have been.

The style of the inner circle of the church as she currently looks, however, is problematic in that it insists there is a folding chair at every table for those who wish to fold themselves into the workings of committees themselves. Ways of giving, organizing, and distributing work and responsibility are all borne of best practices and old habits of generations before. Enough people have stated that the deadliest seven words in the life of the church are "we've never done it that way before," but I'd suggest a second set of dangerous words are "we tried that before and it failed."

Failing Fantastically

A question I've had for years is this: what's so bad about failure? Truly, I understand that we want happiness, sunshine, and daisies for always, but the original church wasn't built on a model of any kind of traditional success. Rather, it was built on the people who came together to try for a more just and loving world. In many ways, the church was built on a radical acceptance of failing in the eyes of the world, sacrificing success for the sake of something more. We follow a man who championed the weakest, the meekest, the most powerless in our midst.

We, as the church, are inhibited by our fears and suffer for it. Our fear keeps us small and skittish, slow to trust, and wary of change. Moving a meeting night is a Herculean task. Changing the worship format is a vital threat. There's a reason new pastors are warned to not change anything for at least six months into their tenure: it is because change is seen as so scary that congregations will turn on you. This last is more myth than fact, but there is something worth noticing about the fact that the myth persists at all.

It isn't that millennials arrive without fear. Rather, they arrive with a different set of fears, perhaps even opposite fears. They fear stagnation, limitation, and spaces where they are not able to create. It is not hard to see why this meets with such derision and conflict in so many traditional institutional churches.

That said, millennials have become ultimately scrappy in their need to cobble together a professional and personal life that ascribes meaning to nontraditional lifestyles. We move amongst jobs, geographies, and relationships with great alacrity. A higher prioritization on freedom than stability manifests throughout our lives, but nowhere is it more obvious than in our employment patterns. Could meetings built on the values of freedom and expression still accomplish the work of the church? Perhaps.

More so than an issue of style, it is the substance of church inner circles that meets with such disruption when encountering millennials. The millennial worldview requires the ability to cocreate a new reality out of remnants of promises not kept, to step into an insecure future from an insecure past. Sacred disruption is a key element of the invitation Christ extends to each of us.

There are big, memorable moments of disruption in the story of Christ. Chasing the moneylenders from the temple springs readily to mind; this is the key moment of Christ losing it in a glorious way on those who would use the temple for purposes other than that which God designed, and has almost reached caricature status in our culture. "Flipping tables" has become slang regarding the need to make a radical shift, at least among the sub-sub-subculture that is clergy millennials. It's doing what needs to be done, and doing it now because it can't wait another moment, let alone another generation.

Matthew 21:12–17 (NRSV)

Jesus Cleanses the Temple

12 *Then Jesus entered the temple and drove out all who were selling and buying in the temple, and he overturned the tables of the money changers and the seats of those who sold doves.* 13 *He said to them, "It is written,*

'My house shall be called a house of prayer';
but you are making it a den of robbers."

14 *The blind and the lame came to him in the temple, and he cured them.* 15 *But when the chief priests and the scribes saw the amazing things that he did, and heard the children crying out in the temple, "Hosanna to the Son of David," they became angry* 16 *and said to him, "Do you hear what these are saying?" Jesus said to them, "Yes; have you never read,*

*'Out of the mouths of infants and nursing babies
you have prepared praise for yourself?'"*

What is particularly fascinating about this moment of Scripture is the use of the phrase "Jesus cleanses the temple." To cleanse is to return to a former state, not to build a new one. It means to renew by rediscovering the former glory. When we cleanse our homes or our bodies, we don't attempt to change the house or body itself, but rather remove the dust and dirt which appear as a natural course of human existence. Here, Jesus is disruptive, but he's disruptive of that which has gone awry, not of the original system itself. He doesn't want the temple gone; he wants the temple restored.

There are smaller moments of holy disruption throughout Scripture as well, and the smaller moments are, arguably, the very substance of Christ. His willingness to engage with the outcasts, to receive critique from a woman who he previously compared to a dog, and to rupture expectations of what can and cannot happen on the Sabbath: this is what makes him memorable. This is also what makes him a threat. For in Christ we see a model agitator who both recognizes the problems of the society he lives in and a tenacity that means he won't let the problems out of his teeth until they are changed. In a season where millennials and social justice activists of various generations are frequently accused of being unable to give it a rest, it is vital the church understand our original model was absolutely terrible at giving it a rest. You think your niece or grandson going on about systemic racism at every family gathering is being insufferable? Just wait until you meet Jesus. He lived and breathed resistance. And while I'm hopeful he took the occasional Sabbath, it is unquestionably meaningful that the stories about him which endure are the ones in which he is being a holy disruption.

Bringing Holy Disruption Home

A move into a disruption of the substance of church inner circles does require a collective acknowledgment of our insecure past and present; a mind-set of scarcity that clings ferociously to the good old days fails to recognize that the good old days had plenty of struggles of their own. The church has had to confront herself over and over again. Today's struggles about our willingness (or unwillingness) to participate as sanctuary spaces for refugees or undocumented immigrants are yesterday's struggles about whether we belong on the front lines of the Civil Rights movement or the anti-war efforts, back to the struggle of whether we belong in the abolitionist movement, and on and on and on. Back and back it goes, wherein the needs of humanity come in direct confrontation with the perceived scarcity of the church's desire to protect herself in her current form. The good old days were rough too.

Furthermore, boomers, raised by the Greatest Generation, were largely instilled with post-war and post-Depression-era values of saving, storing, reusing, and presuming scarcity will return. This can be tremendously helpful in finding ways to last in a throwaway culture, and preservation of tradition is an integral part of the church. It is only when this scarcity mind-set emphasizes fear of what might be lost when something new is attempted (versus hazarding hope on what might be gained) that it becomes a deeply myopic read of the church.

By holding steadfastly to a view of the past with rose-colored glasses, we lose the opportunity for connection across generational experiences of struggle—including the unique struggles faced by millennials at present. If honest conversations about the struggles faced by each could find air to breathe, perhaps we wouldn't spend quite so much time talking past one another.

Instead, we cling to a past that never truly was and devalue the experiences and struggles of the next generation, causing deep and hard-to-repair disconnection. Honesty about our shared frailty and failings might invite new relationships, new levels of exchange, and an openness to receiving the wisdom of those who have been here before. Finding the courage to meet with vulnerability might allow us to become the church.

A more honest appraisal of where we've been and are would reveal internal struggles felt by each generation. Far from making us glum, this should, I hope, prove reassuring. It can renew the sense that we are all in this human experience together, regardless of how broad our differences may appear. It can assuage our panicky sense of isolation, and it can affirm the joy of walking the path together. If we came from there and landed here, who knows where the next leap of faith might take us.

A word of caution along the way: let's resist tokenizing anyone in the church. Just as it would be appalling to ask one person of color to speak for and represent all people of color on our church diversity outreach committee, don't ask one millennial (or boomer, or Gen Xer) to represent their generational peers. We're as diverse as every other generation, and strict representation isn't particularly resonant with the ways of the church. Remember that Christ didn't go for strictly structured sociological diversity in his disciples. He took who was available. He took those who would follow.

Fishing in New Waters

These earliest brothers to the movement of Christ experienced what I hope those of us in love with the church might one day feel: standing perfectly still and realizing we're fishing in whole new waters. Let the impossible become possible in Christ.

Which all sounds lovely, but let's get practical here: How will the community function without committees? It's a fair question. It will involve a relinquishing of control and a re-centering of trust. It will involve experimentation with leaderless movements and investment of time in more open dialogue. It will most assuredly require us to hold our feelings with less fragility, center voices from the margins, and accept the distinct likelihood of experiencing failure. I have confidence that it can be done. In the end, the community can function with a new form because we've done it before.

Change is inevitable and essential, and Christ can call even the least cooperative waters to yield all kinds of fish. Perhaps the community of church with a less restrictive sense of inner circles will be as simple and world-changing as this:

> *When he had finished speaking, he said to Simon, "Put out into the deep water and let down your nets for a catch."* [5]*Simon answered, "Master, we have worked all night long but have caught nothing. Yet if you say so, I will let down the nets."*

CHAPTER 3

Judas Iscariot the Irreplaceable and the Radical Othering of Self

Help! There is a Millennial in My Pulpit, and other alternative chapter titles for the pages that follow.

All right, step one, friends, is don't panic. We're going to get through this together. Is this rogue millennial in the pulpit threatening any other sacred norms of your community? Are they oddly dressed, pierced, or making their gender less than 100 percent obvious to you? I kid. I don't really think that the vast majority of parishioners of any age would go into true existential crisis over the presence of a millennial in the pulpit (ditto anyone who isn't 50 +, heterosexual, white, married, cisgendered, and male in the pulpit). Or at least I hope they'd have the good sense to recognize that such an outlook is ugly and destructive. If you think you might squirm at someone preaching to you who, as I've often been described "doesn't look like a pastor," maybe do a little soul-searching on that front. How those early fishermen turned fishers of men must have reeked! Jesus would let just about anybody up there to share the word. Here's hoping anyway.

But a millennial in the pulpit can be darn scary because it means that on any given Sunday, you might be expected to listen to or (gasp!) participate in the kind of radical othering of self that is *de rigueur* for this generation.

Drawing our eyes to the challenging aspects of Scripture in our own lived realities is homiletical bread and butter for a new generation of preachers. These preachers are trained to eschew the "three points and a poem" style of preaching, so expect a more vociferous call to Scripture-in-action—personal and particular and even political, local and yet globally aware. Expect to have systems of injustice pointed out to you. Expect to squirm with questions about just how relatable this Judas fellow might be.

Matthew 26:1–16 (NIV)

The Plot Against Jesus

When Jesus had finished saying all these things, he said to his disciples, 2 "As you know, the Passover is two days away—and the Son of Man will be handed over to be crucified."

3 Then the chief priests and the elders of the people assembled in the palace of the high priest, whose name was Caiaphas, 4 and they schemed to arrest Jesus secretly and kill him. 5 "But not during the festival," they said, "or there may be a riot among the people."

Jesus Anointed at Bethany

6 While Jesus was in Bethany in the home of Simon the Leper, 7 a woman came to him with an alabaster jar of very expensive perfume, which she poured on his head as he was reclining at the table.

8 When the disciples saw this, they were indignant. "Why this waste?" they asked. 9 "This perfume could have been sold at a high price and the money given to the poor."

10 Aware of this, Jesus said to them, "Why are you bothering this woman? She has done a beautiful thing to me. 11 The poor you will always have with you, but you will not always have me. 12 When she poured this perfume on my body, she did it to prepare me for burial. 13 Truly I tell you, wherever this gospel is preached throughout the world, what she has done will also be told, in memory of her."

Let's begin with the following assertion: somebody had to be Judas. He is irreplaceable in this familiar story. Christ's final hours are all the more painful to consider by us on the outside, well aware that there is a betrayer among his beloved. According to Matthew, Judas acted of his own volition:

14 *Then one of the Twelve—the one called Judas Iscariot—went to the chief priests* **15** *and asked, "What are you willing to give me if I deliver him over to you?" So they counted out for him thirty pieces of silver.* **16** *From then on Judas watched for an opportunity to hand him over.*

But according to Luke, Satan was in the mix:

Judas Agrees to Betray Jesus

Now the Festival of Unleavened Bread, called the Passover, was approaching, **2** *and the chief priests and the teachers of the law were looking for some way to get rid of Jesus, for they were afraid of the people.* **3** *Then Satan entered Judas, called Iscariot, one of the Twelve.* **4** *And Judas went to the chief priests and the officers of the temple guard and discussed with them how he might betray Jesus.* **5** *They were delighted and agreed to give him money.* **6** *He consented, and watched for an opportunity to hand Jesus over to them when no crowd was present.* (Luke 22:1–6)

These verses represent a shifting and massive idea which, in just a few short phrases, makes a significant difference. Was Judas blithely acting of his own accord, or had he been infected by outside forces, or, option C as it ever was, did Judas wrestle the evil within, a potential that is possessed by each of us?

The first choice is the most straightforward. We tend to like the concept of free will, and if Judas was so willfully malevolent as all this, he becomes a very easy-to-hate villain. If he was driven by an outside force, the whole crucifixion moves from the person-based to the cosmic and pushes us to wonder just what kind of games God is playing at here. It leaves more questions than answers, which might be why we preachers stay away from Luke's iteration since we'd have to attempt to understand and explain the function of Satan as a figure in Scripture. Option C is, to my thinking, the most compelling and the most dangerous because it posits the possibility that any one of us could have been the Judas. If that kind of misguidedness-turned-betrayal-turned-outright-cruelty could come from someone who spent so many of his days with Christ, who's to say it wouldn't or couldn't come up in any one of us? Acknowledging our own capacity for evil is a painful but necessary part of recognizing ourselves in our full humanity.

Evil within or evil from without, either way, the story doesn't work without a Judas. Judas presents the counter-narrative that makes the main story make sense. Without the betrayal of the closest of chosen kin, the sting of Christ's death loses the sharpness that keeps it omnipresent to our senses. This isn't an original argument, but it is one that bears revisiting. It forces us into the least comfortable question in the world: Under what circumstances would I sell out Christ? More to the point, under what circumstances *have I sold Christ out already?*

And, if I'm being totally honest, I sometimes get it. I think I might have been right there with Judas in shock and outrage that Christ allows a woman to waste 300 denarii worth of perfume on his dusty feet rather than spending it to feed the poor. I would have been mightily disappointed at thinking I understood what this guy was preaching and I liked it a lot, only to discover that I had him and his message confused. I might have pushed back.

Judas's issue seems to mainly hinge on a sense of original disruption: just when he thinks he's pinned down what Jesus is about, Jesus changes again. And while the appeals of Judas appear to have no impact on Jesus whatsoever, Judas's expression of dismay leaves me feeling squirmy. Jesus can because Jesus is, but how often do I waste resources when that money could be used to feed the poor?

But more than just the guy who calls out the ridiculous when he sees it, Judas is the disciple most intensely wrestling with his own identity. Friend? Follower? Leader? Part of the system or beyond it? Conspirator or character foil? It had to have been a profound spiritual journey for each of them, weaving closer to Christ and further from the world as they had left it behind. Judas seems particularly at sea as he works to integrate his understanding of the life before with his calling to follow an enigmatic man who doesn't follow the rules.

It's tempting, easy, and convenient to just make Judas a villain. A scapegoat to hate frees us from having to engage with the complexity of every person, so if we can just reduce Judas to the size of a Disney villain, he presents no real existential threat to our spiritual experience. We get the satisfaction of the miserable end to his story without having to wrestle with the genuine tragedy of suicide.

We paint Judas as the villain and are glad when he is gone because it is the simpler path and one that least forces us to confront our own Judas-esque struggles in identity, path, morality, and loyalty. If he's just a bad guy, then we share no culpability in his errors. His cruelty is his alone to bear, and bear it he does. Acknowledging Judas as more complicated than a straightforward villain would push us to acknowledge him and ourselves as flawed, as desperately in need of grace as Judas himself was in those final hours.

Scripture gives us plenty of bad guys (and gals) to run counter to Christ, so I don't believe we need Judas to be a villain, so much as we need Judas to act as Christ's only real foil. A foil is a much more finicky figure than a villain, for a foil shares some characteristics with the heroine or hero, and that pushes some deeply uncomfortable comparisons. Do we dare consider then that Judas shared characteristics with Christ? And one step further, do we recognize the ways in which we share experiences with both of them?

Judas and Christ are not so polar opposite as it would be convenient to believe them to be. Both are men on a journey, seeking the path of righteousness. Christ has a strong advantage on that one, but to declare Judas as without faith is to discount his whole presence in the story of Christ and his disciples. Both men proclaim a value on taking care of the poor, the sick, the lonely, and lost. Both face the challenges of living in community and actively resisting the law even to their own potential peril. Judas isn't so far afield as a villain after all.

Take Us to Church

It seems that Judas Iscariot was on a journey of spiritual self-discovery. Not unlike millennials, Judas is trying to find his spot in this overarching narrative that doesn't appear to speak to him where he is, at least not at first blush. He is drawn away from a safe faith that requires little of him and into the space of deeper understanding and chaos. More than once, he seems ill at ease and a bit out of place, though it is hard to imagine anyone joining the community of disciples and not feeling that way. Judas seems to be wrestling with attempting to understand Jesus, so frequently enigmatic and so open, while reconciling with the world around them.

As millennials wend their way to and from the life of any specific spiritual community, they are wrestling with personal spiritual identity. While previous generations stood much more firmly in fixed identities—Christian, churchgoer, constancy—millennials speak a language of personal faith identity and experiences. Identity is more fluid than ever before, and this naturally meets with resistance in settings where fixed identities help us navigate the world.

The temptation to cast this as one more manifestation of millennial self-obsession is strong and understandable. I won't deny that an element of that exists, and all of us would be wise to reject the role of the church as a tailor-made, self-centered journey: worship as the "me" hour. We have enough "me" hours, or at least enough options for them. But in a culture of self-care, let's consider including a "we" hour, centering on care for the community and a chance to radically "other" ourselves.

I think perhaps millennials are equipped to help us consider a "we" hour that centralizes the experiences of others. I see potential in millennial spiritual journeying as a path toward this radical self-othering and one of potentially tremendous value in the life of the church.

I Don't Want to Radical Anything, Let Alone Myself

To radically other the self is a funny turn of phrase. To "other" as a verb has a long tradition in critical theory and refers to the lines we draw to differentiate between people. Specifically, othering serves to harm by establishing a set of values that normalize a singular set of experiences. By putting men, for example, or whiteness at the center, we effectively turn everyone who isn't that into an "other." They cease to be themselves and start being defined as "not me."

To "other" the self, then, involves a bit of chameleonic imagination. Rather than simply pretending to be in a category that we are not, we instead must try to shift our internal perspective away from holding ourselves at the center of every story. It can happen when we ask ourselves why girls are described as cute and sweet while boys are declared strong and brave. We can shift our perspective when white people ask themselves the last piece of literature they read by a Black author, or what their regular encounters with persons of color entail. It happens every time we reposition ourselves from the starring role, and ask ourselves whose voices, experiences, and lives we have failed to understand because we were too busy worrying about what it all meant for us. We might consider the ways in which the story isn't about us or isn't about what we thought it would be at all. We might attempt to see out from behind the eyes of Judas.

Don't let the word radical worry you—it isn't prescriptive or political. Radical simply is what Christ calls us to be from the very beginning.

Radical just names what is already there: the sheer wildness of giving up what is known, comfortable, safe, and easy, for that which cracks open the possibility of the fullness of humanity. If we move away from making ourselves the center of every story, we move in an inherently radical direction. And a radical direction such as this one requires us to breathe new air, with the promise that it is in such a new air that we find our fullest selves, and Christ waiting to welcome us.

CHAPTER 4

Thomas and Un-curated Faith in the Snapchat Generation

John 20:19-29 (NRSV)

Jesus Appears to His Disciples

19On the evening of that first day of the week, when the disciples were together, with the doors locked for fear of the Jewish leaders, Jesus came and stood among them and said, "Peace be with you!" 20After he said this, he showed them his hands and side. The disciples were overjoyed when they saw the Lord.

21Again Jesus said, "Peace be with you! As the Father has sent me, I am sending you." 22And with that he breathed on them and said, "Receive the Holy Spirit. 23If you forgive anyone's sins, their sins are forgiven; if you do not forgive them, they are not forgiven."

Jesus Appears to Thomas

24Now Thomas (also known as Didymus), one of the Twelve, was not with the disciples when Jesus came. 25So the other disciples told him, "We have seen the Lord!"

Thomas and Un-curated Faith

But he said to them, "Unless I see the nail marks in his hands and put my finger where the nails were, and put my hand into his side, I will not believe."

26A week later his disciples were in the house again, and Thomas was with them. Though the doors were locked, Jesus came and stood among them and said, "Peace be with you!" 27Then he said to Thomas, "Put your finger here; see my hands. Reach out your hand and put it into my side. Stop doubting and believe."

28Thomas said to him, "My Lord and my God!"

29Then Jesus told him, "Because you have seen me, you have believed; blessed are those who have not seen and yet have believed."

What Am I Doing with My Life? Or, Sunday Afternoon in the Pastor's Study

I had preached one of *those* sermons. The ones that feel at once like they wrote themselves and like they took everything but your last breath to move from your heart to the page and from the page to the people. There is a feeling that comes for a lot of preachers when a sermon just has to be preached and, on its way out of our mouths, it stops feeling like we are doing the speaking. Call it the Spirit, call it an out-of-body experience, call it whatever you like. It is the sensation that there really is something to ministering, to shepherding the word into the world. I was elated and exhausted for the rest of the service, grateful for a skillful musical director, an enthusiastic congregation, and strong lay leadership, which meant the rest of our time together that morning was a shared responsibility. I made my post-benediction, pre-postlude exit as usual to the only space to which the architecture funneled people—the snack table—and poured myself a cup of juice, attempting to regain my sense of voice and breath before the onslaught of post-worship interactions to which my introverted self has never developed a real level of comfort. There, a longtime member was setting out a small feast for the impending crowd. She looked me dead in the eyes, referenced the title of the postlude song (which I'm sure I had approved the week before but was completely off my radar at the moment), and said with disgust, "That was just an abomination." Of course I don't remember what I preached that day. I don't remember anything except that comment, puncturing the feeling that I'd left it all on the table or in the pulpit as it were, and my subsequent self-interrogation: Is anything I'm doing making the slightest bit of difference here? My answer, at least that day: I doubt it.

Though funny in the long view as that one time a choice I made got to "abomination" status, it immediately crystallized a deep and abiding doubt. It is a doubt with which far too many clergy, regardless of generation, wrestle. It is the question of whether we are making any real impact at all. And no, our sense of the worth of the work should not be so easily unsettled as all this, yet I wonder if that sense of doubt can be, in the end, our salvation.

Doubt: So Hot Right Now

Doubt is having a moment. Or at least, it was about ten to fifteen years ago. Doubt was seen for a season as the next big hipster movement of the church, and a healthy embrace of good old-fashioned doubt is beneficial for most of us. Overconfidence in our own interpretations, statutes, and systems is hardly the way of Christ. On the level of personal faith, I don't think I know a single preacher who hasn't wrestled with, or outright rejected, the historical veracity of the Jesus story as Scripture describes it. Too much has happened, too much has been left out, too much has been done to the story. Giving doubt a home in faith is an act of courage. It provides room for exploration of the possibility that there may yet be some truth if we can excavate it from the weight of doctrine. Doubt has become so hip that we've sanitized it, but dear Didymus (another nickname for Thomas which translates to "the twin") was not swinging in on some fresh trend of hipster unbelief.

Thomas was not posing for Caravaggio in *The Incredulity of Saint Thomas*, a painting that I (and I imagine many others) have been finding creepy for quite some time. This image frequently accompanies the story of Thomas, featuring Christ baring his chest and side while several disciples look on, and a particular figure (presumably Thomas), with his arm guided by the hand of another, inserting his finger into the side-wound of a placid and invitational-looking Christ. "Incredulity" is a comically sanitized way of describing what's going on in this painting, as it suggests instead a doubt so strong that Thomas would actually invade the body of Christ to have said doubt satisfied.

This expression of doubt was not posturing. Dear Didymus did what any rational human being would do—he believed his dead friend was dead. When Caravaggio then conceptualized a moment of nearly clinical curiosity, it seems he missed some of the deeply felt power of the resurrection narrative: that all of us would be, should be, and *are* in total shock, fear, and awe at the revelation that the dead man lives.

Thomas's doubt speaks volumes because it tells a truth that we never seem to say out loud in church—that this crucible moment of our faith, Christ's resurrection—is a deeply crazy thing to believe in. We must stop pretending that having the majority in numbers makes our faith system any more logical than the beliefs of any other group. Don't let banality lead to a numbed understanding of what we're saying. A man was crucified, dead, and buried. On the third day, he rose from the dead. That's an insane thing to claim.

We fear the things we doubt because we might commit the grave sin of being wrong. Or looking foolish. Or poking our fingers around in the wounds of the dead brought back to life. We might get the confirmation we seek and then—horror of horrors—be compelled to act. We might become the object of derisive laughter. We might be mistaken. So we operate under faith that isn't quite blind, but isn't quite honest either, at least not until we settle into our own understandable doubts. Thomas speaks to us out of our past because he says what most of us are thinking: "I don't buy it. I can't believe it."

Note that Christ invites Thomas to have a poke around in his wounds, but it does not follow that Thomas actually did so (these are the stories we tell ourselves in art and writing and life to add color and . . . depth. Gruesome.) For some reason, the words of Christ seem more than enough for Thomas. Yet they seem to be insufficient for us on this end of history, and our insatiable need to portray a more invasive manifestation of doubt.

Thomas gets dismissed for this behavior way too easily—doubting Thomas being an infectious strain of derision in our common vocabulary. Yet I think he might just exist to be our own Didymus—our twin. He shows us who we are when our pretexts are stripped away by shock. I see here a parallel to this intense, immediate self-expression with the expression of doubt by Thomas. He wasn't posing for a painting. He was wrestling with the impossible in real time. Not entirely unlike a teenager encountering their life on Snapchat. Stay with me here.

The nature of doubt is a slippery thing. It keeps us safe, distant, aloof in ways that are actually helpful to our survival. Are those leftovers safe to eat? Doubting it could save you a bout of food poisoning. Reasonable doubt and the mysterious space beyond it is what theoretically keeps our justice system moving. Doubt might not be the opposite of faith, but the opposite of arrogance.

Arrogance is the surety that one is both seen and admired, that we are a focal point to another person's day. Doubt says the terrifying opposite: we might not be important at all. There is a balance to be found in this, as in most things. As I've reassured countless nervous middle schoolers: no one is thinking about you as much as you are. I think a healthier position for ego is knowing that most of us are somewhat solipsistic creatures who are working on it, taking active steps to make sure we see and hear others. It makes sense that the wrestling match between our arrogance and doubt would yield some deeply chaotic manifestations in the no-editor-needed technology of today, but doubt is absolutely present.

More than just understandable, doubt might be useful. Bear in mind that Thomas, the oh-so-doubtful apostle, is said to have gone on to spread the gospel far and wide, beyond even the reaches of the Roman Empire, going so far as India to bear the word to others. Christ doesn't disempower or dismiss him for expressing some doubt. Even though he wasn't quick to recognize or trust in the resurrected Christ, Jesus chose to send him.

Seeking Confirmation

There is a strong and trendy belief that young people are shallow (as every generation has thought of the generation coming up after them). The selfie-stick generation with every possible filter, self-deleting photo streams, stories curated within an inch of their lives—they do not know how to be real. They hide behind the technology that allows the world to see them only in the best of light.

But look past the steady stream of Instagrammed moments and tabulations of likes to determine which version of the truth stays and which disappears, and see a new epistemology growing across generations: a deep and abiding need to see and be seen, to know and be known, and a vulnerability in expressing doubt that is deeply refreshing because of its honesty.

The millennial generation is, in some ways, brave and honest about doubt. We doubt our visibility to those who love us, and so we plaster ourselves everywhere. We doubt our lovability unless externally confirmed through likes and retweets. We feel invisible if we lack constant validation that we are being seen. We mistrust our relationships if there's a decrease of responses to our snap-stories. Our substance is encapsulated in that which is visible.

That might sound vulgar and a bit sad, but it's the natural conclusion of humanity's vulnerability when mixed with instantaneous communication. I'd wager that our whole history has involved some semblance of this same phenomenon, this unimaginable need to see ourselves reflected in the eyes and hearts of those around us. As a species, we have constantly relied on feedback to assess our safety, our roles, and our potential. It's just that our means and methods of communication have gotten so much bigger, faster, and all-consuming. All the filters in the world won't save us from being unable to filter ourselves away from our own humanity.

But really, thank God. For in needing to confront our own humanity—doubt and all—we come closest to seeing what Christ was up to: celebrating the fullness and frailty of the human experience. Therefore doubt is part of what makes us human, and it is our humanity expressed in Christ that can save us.

Firmly rooted in traditions of terrific historical significance, consciousness-raising is a piece of every great social movement and personal revelation. There are elements of both the personal and private to raising awareness within all public revelations of need. For anything to change, we ourselves must become aware. We must raise consciousness—in both ourselves and in others. To become conscious, particularly on a systemic level, necessitates holding multiple perspectives at once. We must see ourselves in the story and understand ourselves as a part in a larger system. Only by doing so can we hope to experience and effect change. Could there be a more plain expression of seeking a place in the story than millennial communication? Our curated stories hyper-communicate where we locate ourselves or wish to locate ourselves in the story of our lives. We are constantly narrative-building and attempting to highlight that our story exists and our place in it matters. This may not resemble consciousness-raising in any traditional sense in that the end goal may not be community-wide awareness-building of a social need. Instead, I envision these modalities as a path for millennials to consciousness-raise within the self.

Consider the possibility of Instagram or Snapchat or Twitter as modes of reflexivity for millennials. To be reflexive is to take reflection one step further by seeing first what is there to be seen, and then to consider how it is that we come to see it in such a way. It means to consider the knowledge and worldviews we possess, and how they came to be shaped that way, rather than just presuming that what is reflected is the absolute truth or an accurate representation of a singular reality. Is much of the use of social media vapid and about instant gratification? Sure. But in the midst of all of the reactionary nonsense that goes on, there is a simultaneous force of self-examination that comes through looking so intensely and considering so deeply how the world might be seeing you.

Of course, it goes well beyond the millennials and beyond simple technological experience. Rather, the technology available is just the latest mode of expressing this deep, internal, and perennial need. From Polaroid pictures to daguerreotypes to portraiture, we have long desired to see ourselves affixed to the story. With today's technology, the most susceptible among us to trends experience the influence well before we're sure how to use it or even what it is that these new capabilities enable and expose. The humanity and self-doubt skates right on the surface for millennials.

Rather than hand-wringing about it, what if we took these millennial communication patterns as a gift? What if these millennials are unveiling for us the chasm of doubt that plagued Thomas and plagues us all, and witnessed this as an opportunity to present a more Christlike response? Go for it, Thomas. Poke, press, interrogate the reality of my love for you. I'll be here. I'll wait.

This is our consciousness newly raised, our sense of deepest possible joy, or gravest doubt, for Scripture does not indicate that Thomas actually poked around in the wounds of Christ. That's part of the fictional reimagining of the story of Thomas; that he had to touch those wounds, a level of doubt that would cross the threshold from incredulity to invasive. The words and visible wounds were enough to reassure him that it was safe to believe.

The Relief of Being Well-liked

Thomas was not, I think, attempting to invite controversy. He just knew that the intimacy of first-person knowledge was the only thing that could reassure him of the impossible—that God spoke truly, that Christ would return. The expression of "My Lord and my God!" from Thomas is the exhalation of fear mixed with the exultation of knowing your love, your faith, and your hope were never in vain. It may be woefully diminishing to compare this to the tiny heart notification on your Instagram feed, even when its source is an earthly beloved, but on some level they speak to the same truth: we are longing to be loved. In Thomas and the millennials, that love is expressed.

So perhaps millennials operate on a similar frame—just with an exhausting scope of global fame or infamy at the fingertips of anyone at all. Their presence is marked by their own insistence on being visible, noted, and, when possible, celebrated. Or at least their presence is marked and hopes to be minimally derided. If they can be seen and known, fully expressing humanity and betraying their insecurities and doubts, they can be reassured of love.

These young people, then, might just be wrestling with the impossible in real time—how much to share, how much to keep, how to be seen as our best self. They are encountering life through filters, and they do so at incredible personal risk. The infectious nature of bullying emboldened by the anonymity of the Internet is widely public, yet we don't seem to have many great ideas on what to do about it. Every tweet risks a clap back, every post risks wallowing in the emptiness of non-response or the harsh critique of those who wish to tear down. I don't believe that we have a sudden influx of bullying impulses or behavior in our culture, merely that we have been freed of the consequences of seeing the weight of our actions face-to-face. Anonymity begets cruelty when left unchecked, and any millennial knows this to be true. No matter how focused one is in their attempts to protect their social media footprint, there is no real safe quarter on the internet, and so the risk of calling attention to oneself is incredibly high.

We have to ask ourselves, then, why do millennials do it, living their lives online? What's the value in pinning our sense of self-worth on the reactionary impulses of our invisible peers? Are they just gluttons for punishment? Perhaps so. Or perhaps there might there be something deeper at work: a public exorcism of the demons of doubt, lived out on a global yet personal stage. They are reckoning with the personal in a public fashion and who's to say any previous generation wouldn't have done the exact same thing given the same technology. Perhaps then, the Snapchat generation is all of us, back to Thomas if not before, struggling with balancing our doubts and our faith, wanting above all to be reassured that what we hope for could be true.

CHAPTER 5

The Great Commission and the Global Generation

Matthew 14:22–33 (NIV)

Jesus Walks on the Water

²²Immediately Jesus made the disciples get into the boat and go on ahead of him to the other side, while he dismissed the crowd. ²³After he had dismissed them, he went up on a mountainside by himself to pray. Later that night, he was there alone, ²⁴and the boat was already a considerable distance from land, buffeted by the waves because the wind was against it.

²⁵Shortly before dawn Jesus went out to them, walking on the lake. ²⁶When the disciples saw him walking on the lake, they were terrified. "It's a ghost," they said, and cried out in fear.

²⁷But Jesus immediately said to them: "Take courage! It is I. Don't be afraid."

²⁸"Lord, if it's you," Peter replied, "tell me to come to you on the water."

²⁹"Come," he said.

The Great Commission and the Global Generation

Then Peter got down out of the boat, walked on the water and came toward Jesus. 30But when he saw the wind, he was afraid and, beginning to sink, cried out, "Lord, save me!"

31Immediately Jesus reached out his hand and caught him. "You of little faith," he said, "why did you doubt?"

32And when they climbed into the boat, the wind died down. 33Then those who were in the boat worshiped him, saying, "Truly you are the Son of God."

Matthew 28:16–20 (NRSV)

The Great Commission

16Then the eleven disciples went to Galilee, to the mountain where Jesus had told them to go. 17When they saw him, they worshiped him; but some doubted. 18 hen Jesus came to them and said, "All authority in heaven and on earth has been given to me. 19Therefore go and make disciples of all nations, baptizing them in the name of the Father and of the Son and of the Holy Spirit, 20and teaching them to obey everything I have commanded you. And surely I am with you always, to the very end of the age."

After a long sleepless flight, border control, and hauling a gigantic suitcase across London by tube, I was sweaty, exhausted, and about done with the travel adventure. The requisite wrong turns of the geographically-declined put behind me, I was less than encouraged when I found the dead-end street containing my home for the summer: a series of warehouses. Billed as communal living spaces for artists, I had sublet a space in the warehouse online from a lovely young woman who happened to be a professional clown. It seemed whimsical and fun for a twenty-something and a summer abroad, particularly given that I was there to work on human trafficking issues and could use some fun to return home to.

But as I wrestled my suitcase to the entryway (door is a bit generous), I was having my doubts. Luckily, a couple was out front and pointed me on my way up several more flights of stairs into what was an only slightly cleaner version of *Rent*.

So it was that in the summer of 2011, I lived in a warehouse in London. Moving in with painters, musicians, and literal clowns, I became a resident chaplain of sorts. I was there to do anti-human-trafficking work as a volunteer with an international nonprofit but became a de facto living confessional booth for this motley crew from all corners of the UK, as well as Spain, Hungary, Australia, New Zealand, the US, and elsewhere. Musicians and photographers, dancers and actors, guerilla street artists and painters, and more clowns than I ever thought I'd encounter on a daily basis. Different races, genders, sexual orientations, and while minimal on the faith front, they were robustly diverse. My faith identity seemed as much a source of curiosity as a source of discomfort to anyone, at least no more off-putting than all the clowning was to me.

This experience ruptured many of my preconceived notions of family, home, place, and community. Across language barriers and countries of origin and life experiences, family dinners became a norm. We'd gather around a large table and bring food and stories to share. It took me a while to find my voice in a place full of such fascinating and full characters as these, but they provided a space at the table for me. Eventually, in ones and twos, they began to come to me with a funny kind of confession. "Do you think you could pray with me?" they would ask in hushed tones, the desire for prayer as the confession itself. So, we prayed. Over heartbreak in relationships, pregnancy scares, and drug addictions. Over the identity crises of millennial lives and unsure futures and painful, passionate dedication to creations that might never be appreciated by another soul. It was disruptive to my sense of who these voyagers were and why I had presumed so much about their spirituality.

Furthermore, it disrupted my sense that all travel was born of privilege. Knowing that my sojourns to India and South Africa and Palestine/Israel and so forth were all possible through the generosity of those I love was a reminder of my privilege. Furthermore, that my freedom to travel comes at the cost of having a US passport and a culture/religion that doesn't limit my solo travel were also truths I held as sharp reminders of power I never earned. Knowing that my skin color and marital status and gender were not inhibiting my mobility, and that this was for utterly arbitrary reasons—where and to whom I was born—meant that I had extraordinary freedom, a fact of which I tended to be (and continue to be) hyper-conscious.

Yet here, in this warehouse of rooms that leaked and makeshift stairs and ever-occupied bathrooms, were a group of nomads who followed their art. I've got as much Midwestern Protestant work ethic as the next person. I have spent years attempting to disentangle my identity from my productivity. Even I had to admit there was something past charming and into the realm of the sublime about these millennials living on toast and cheap wine for the sake of creating what they felt called to create. They and their drive to create could not be contained or fixed to one location.

This culture of mobility was somewhat new to me as new people moved in and out of the warehouse rooms with remarkable frequency. I didn't know it could be like that. I knew many of my friends and I had scattered geographically after school or from our hometowns, but that seemed so normal as to be invisible to me. Perhaps this was because those travels were generally laced up in the trappings of respectable reasons—a new job, grad school, etc. I was aware of the concept of mission trips, though I didn't attend my first one until I was leading them as a solo pastor. I'd spent time on a self-directed service pilgrimage in India for a season, but in these people, I became aware of something new that was happening to my generation—they were living a missionary life.

The missionary life got well warped by colonialism and we can't talk about mission without acknowledging that weight. With our white savior complexes, missionaries carry the pall of destruction as a mantle historically deserved by all white Christianity in the US. We carried out the mission of cultural destruction and the imposition of our own norms for the sake of enveloping others to look like Christ the Anglo-American. But the original sense of mission lives on, persisting through our faults, in the Great Commission to go and seek others. Mission is evangelism in which we have the awesome burden and joy of carrying something inside of us—the greatest of news—and feel compelled down to our core to go forth and share it with others. Christ's original commission was never about collecting the most converts or scaring people into spiritual submission. It was about recognizing how good this news is, so good that it would be criminal to keep it to ourselves. And it is just such a missionary life that I think these warehouse kids—all of us—were seeking.

Not for Christ, necessarily, but for where their hearts were guiding them. To more art. More painting. More dancing. More philosophizing over wine in the parking lot-turned-terrace. Waking up every day knowing that they had something so good to give the world and a ceaseless drive to go forth and create it, sharing it with anyone, even a geeky recent seminary grad from the suburbs of Chicago.

Millennials on the Move

From where I sit, on any given day and in many given countries, this generation is on the move. Millennials may seem like fish out of water, or at least fishermen and fisherwomen out of the boat. This looks frighteningly precarious to generations where the highest values orbit a principle value of rootedness: long-lasting careers, buying a home, starting a family, being well-insured, and saving for retirement. The more rooted generations are doing the same as millennials: living out the path expected to lead to a high quality of life. These are the steps to happiness.

Generations coming up through world wars and the Great Depression built into our very DNA an appreciation for what it means to be safe and secure. These markers of adulthood are what get us accepted into the club of fully developed human grown-ups, instead of the somewhat condescending moniker of "emerging adults." Over the past few decades, this newer category has become a mild way of naming the disappointment our parents feel when we haven't yet settled down in ways that previous generations did by their early twenties, when we aren't yet married at thirty or having kids at thirty-five, when we still haven't picked just one career. If only we could fall in step with these proven paths to happiness, then the kids would be all right.

Except when they aren't. Except when so many of our generation were raised by divorced parents, by families struggling with bankruptcy and foreclosure, by the unexpected ruptures of layoffs and having to move frequently for work. These given paths don't lead to happiness for all, and maybe they don't lead to happiness even for many. They certainly do not represent the one golden truth on how to seek a fulfilling life.

In these experiences are lessons learned for the millennial generation if we are paying attention. We cannot discount the joy that comes for so many in marriage, in having a long-lasting home, in maintaining a vibrant and multi-decade career. It just might be that this is not our call. Our call, the evidence would suggest, is far closer to one that insists we get up and move, try, progress, and create. Maybe no one articulated a Great Commission just for us, but we've got the first half down. Go forth!

It isn't that millennials have faith any greater than anyone else, but the necessity of acting on faith is becoming increasingly acute. We are a generation with greater, broader mobility than any that came before us. Where migrations once occurred around major crises like droughts, wars, famines, and sweeping social upheaval, they occur now on a much smaller scale. Obscene costs of living squeeze us out of neighborhoods, as gentrification squeezes us into others while pushing out long-time residents. Our dissatisfaction with traditional job practices moves us to creative flexibility and a willingness to let go quickly. We move for myriad reasons: for work, for love, for curiosity, and for a desire to better know the world and ourselves.

And when we go, we step out in faith. We might not call it faith in God or anything of the sort, but we have faith in other things: the general goodness of people regardless of culture, the hospitality of strangers, the impeccability of small disasters turning into small miracles. These are things that travelers from everywhere and going anywhere bond over: our collective faith in the journey.

Stepping Toward, Not Away From

Of course, the Great Commission isn't just to go; it's also to go forth and create disciples of every nation. The impulse to flee, uproot, and hit a self-destruct button on life's problems is a shallow response to the big picture of life. But mobility for the sake of seeking others—connection, family, a possible future yet to be forged—that's a "go forth." Not every millennial is on the move, and not all those on the move are creating disciples in the traditional sense. By stricter definitions, hardly any of them are, including those on so-called mission trips.

Mission trips have extraordinary value when it comes to coalescing a group identity, puncturing sociocultural and theological bubbles, and developing a sense of commitment of time to something beyond ourselves. Mission trips can also be valuable as a starting point for considering issues of systemic injustice. That is, these trips can cause us to ask more than just "what can I do to help at this shelter?" They can move us through the starter questions of "Why does God let some people suffer in ways so much more abject than others?" They can draw us into the heart of the mission issue: "Why do we let people suffer in this way?," "What systems of oppression cause us to need shelters in the first place?," and so forth. Disappearing are the days of using the guise of mission to attempt to colonize the poor or oppressed into a faith system for the sake of upping our conversion count. Thank God for that. Of all the notes Christ gives the disciples on healing the sick, visiting the imprisoned, caring for the widow and orphan: none of these come with a religious cudgel. All of them are marked by simply living out faith.

Perhaps this is what Christ meant actually—not that we go forth and convert strangers to worship of himself, but that we ourselves become transformed through the experience of caring for others. In that case, well done, clever Christ, because that's the exact sort of discipleship I think is most likely to be done.

Relationships are indeed formed on these types of trips—connecting briefly and yet with lasting nodes of contact preserved in social media. When you make airplane friends who end up at your wedding, it is a valuable thing to have ways to intersect your lives and keep in touch with one another. There is a site of potential discipleship in this manifestation of mobility. The way millennials love while mobile looks remarkably like the disciples.

A Model for New Discipleship

The disciples' patterns of life hinged on movement, establishing moments of deep connection, and then moving on. They kept in touch with letters, but the majority of their time was spent in motion. This was not borne out of restlessness but rather necessity—made so both by the culture and by the commission of Christ himself. Turkey, Asia Minor, Syria, North Africa, Ethiopia, India, Greece, Persia and beyond: the disciples got around. They worked to encourage and equip fledgling communities of followers, outrun those who found them outrageous, and shared the gospel like children, spilling a secret too wonderful to keep.

You can't go forth and create at the same time as you stay put and maintain. Can't be done. This is not to say that everyone should go forth and create any more than everyone should stay put and remain. The call to be the church requires valuing the necessity of both those who stay put and those who keep moving.

The church which stays steady, rooted, and unchanging, might forever provide a home church to an uprooted generation. This is a fine and worthy option—be a familiar and safe locale for the youth to return at Christmas, a warehouse storing memories with sufficient consistency to stir up nostalgia for childhoods past while building new stories and memories for the next generation of children who come through the doors. Having a home to return to is psychologically imperative for healthy sojourning.

But the church as a living body cannot simply be that which stays put. It is required to be in kinesis. We call ourselves the body of Christ, and we are called to be a body in motion. The way the story of the Bible and the story of the historical church still breathes life into the world today is through this sense of kinesis: being alive, as represented by our actions. These motions can be as small as gestures and as broad as the globe, and they maintain an internal consistency by celebrating the ways in which we interact and move with, past, and through each other's stories. Our call is to share the good news in word and action, and odds are against a steady stream of new relationships with the world's most vulnerable coming through our door. There is an incompatibility to remaining comfortable in our familiar pews and meeting the needs of the world since the needs don't tend to come to us. Instead, we have to consider how we move out into the world, seeking relationships, seeking God's work and will in the world.

The question then becomes how do we prepare for discipleship and a missionary life regardless of occupation. Missionary life cannot be reserved only for those who can make a full-time living on it. In fact, we might serve better if we disentangle livelihood from the service we provide. Discipleship has to wend its way into the daily fabric of house cleaner and office worker, freelancer and teacher, all of us. The Great Commission was to all of us, so we need to figure out how best to respond in each new generation. How do we millennials make disciples who are prepared to go forth and make disciples of every nation?

New/Old Discipleship, New/Old Mission

Perhaps we begin by de-codifying the rules and roles of Christianity. We tend to treat our rules as restrictions rather than supports to guide a path toward innovative, creative futures. Too often, we fail to think with sufficient breadth and depth about what makes mission.

We try to tame mission into something palatable, safe, and fixed, leaning heavily on that which we can go out and briefly impact rather than those concerns which might require us to change personally. This comes in the form of committees that become too insular and small, or pet projects that go without new consideration or examination for far too long. We think of mission as a place we give money, or a one-week trip, or a line item in the budget. Those who go forth into the field are, if we're feeling brave enough, called missionaries. But mostly, mission remains confined in a box, or around a conference table, or in a slideshow of photos.

What if, instead, we deconstructed mission and instead rallied around this idea that all of life is mission? I don't imagine mission will lose any of its specialness if we normalize it, making it more broadly accessible to all. Or maybe it will, in which case that's a good indication we've been overly precious about it in the first place. If we dismantle the concept of mission teams and social justice agendas and instead push the question of "What is our mission?" as the leading component of every decision and conversation had within the life of a church, we might come closer to living as the disciples did.

Decolonizing our own philosophical and practical approaches to mission, globalization, and our own faith is instrumental to this work. Decolonization refers to the act of recognizing, naming, and disentangling the damage done by centuries of global conquests which are still playing out throughout the world today. It's tempting to think of colonization as a thing of the past when nations big on militaries and low on morality would take dominion over nations and whole continents of people. We want to believe that was something terrible that happened back then at the hands of those people who are nothing like us. But of course, they are us, exactly. And our only hope for affecting change to these long-standing ways of being and mistreating each other is for us to see them and recognize our own complicity within them.

Acted out through genocidal violence and enslavement, the practice of colony-building had and has implications that are social, racial, political, economic, and gendered. The world does not need one more white woman's voice on the ways in which colonization continues, so suffice it to say that these are the foundations on which much of the Western world is built (especially the US) and colonization manifests loudly in the church, and there are many beautifully written books and articles to that effect. To move forward purposefully requires us to reckon with the ways we continue to colonize, including the ways we colonize from the pulpit and colonize the pulpit itself.

We colonize from the pulpit by relying on dogma and simplistic worldviews to feed the loop, reinforcing systems of injustice because to do otherwise would make people uncomfortable. By preaching messages of "we are all one" and "can't we all just get along," we attempt to erase the experiences of so many people. Rendering difference invisible is an act of colonization and one which we use to temper our own disease. Christ's preaching honored the experiences of many, and welcomed the lived experiences of those who came to see him, regardless of where they were from. He didn't use his preaching to perpetuate the norms of an unjust and violent empire. He used his preaching to see the people within that empire and honor their voices and lives. So too must we try to do from the pulpit.

Furthermore, we, the institutional church, colonize the pulpit herself. We treat it as our spiritual duck blind, a place from which we can preach our own truths rather than God's, and accept glory on behalf of our own cleverness along the way. We use the pulpit to receive the affirmations so many in the clergy want and need. We treat the pulpit as a tool or a weapon by which we can defend and attack as we see fit. Until we recognize that the pulpit is neither tool nor weapon, we cannot decolonize her.

The church has had a particularly nasty history with colonization, a convert-or-be-killed (or convert-and-be-enslaved) backstory that we have attempted to soften into the more emotionally violent than overtly physical. Our cruelty has taken the form of paternalistic condescension, attempting to "civilize" other groups into thinking, behaving, and believing as white, Christian, Euro-Americans, though we participated in and perpetuated acts of overt violence as well. While we've come a long way from these dehumanizing practices, we still struggle to find ways to co-create without condescension and to serve without putting ourselves in the role of savior.

We could begin to decolonize the concept of mission by removing the connotations that mission is something *we* go over *there* to do. By centrally locating mission nearby, we can admit with humility that we need as much as anyone else and there is work to be done nearby, as near as our own hearts. That's not to say we never go elsewhere to serve, but that we disentangle our voluntourism from a holy call and our commitment to serve from a desire to exoticize the poverty of others. If we can decolonize our minds and hearts, we can begin to see and attempt to heal some of the damage we, collectively, have done.

Therefore, decolonizing the way we define discipleship gives us room to breathe. In that space of lung expansion, we can breathe the wonderful truth that to seek, find, and love requires neither conference table nor plane ticket. Rather, all our paths are missions and every participant is a disciple.

Practically, the implications are that we necessarily need a more expansive church vocabulary for mission in all its forms; a vocabulary that will match our actions. We need to change the way we think about mission first by moving power dynamics within it, and then we need to change the way we talk about it, by which point we will hopefully be able to change the way we live it.

I think this is what the millennial generation is trying, inadvertently, to teach us. By resisting the confines of any one career, geographic location, or social identity, we incarnate mobility in a way that frees us to seek out the deeper callings of life wherever they might take us next. This is not the simplistic notion of chasing our bliss. This is a return to that which is at our very roots: embodying and enacting what it means to be alive. The church could learn a great deal from this sensibility.

CHAPTER 6

Family of Choice

Matthew 12:46–50 (NRSV)

While Jesus was still talking to the crowd, his mother and brothers stood outside, wanting to speak to him. 47Someone told him, "Your mother and brothers are standing outside, wanting to speak to you."

48He replied to him, "Who is my mother, and who are my brothers?" 49Pointing to his disciples, he said, "Here are my mother and my brothers. 50For whoever does the will of my Father in heaven is my brother and sister and mother."

John 1:43–51 (NRSV)

43The next day Jesus decided to go to Galilee. He found Philip and said to him, "Follow me." 44Now Philip was from Bethsaida, the city of Andrew and Peter. 45Philip found Nathanael and said to him, "We have found him about whom Moses in the law and also the prophets wrote, Jesus son of Joseph from Nazareth." 46Nathanael said to him, "Can anything good come out of Nazareth?" Philip said to him, "Come and see." 47When Jesus saw Nathanael coming toward him, he said of him, "Here is truly an Israelite in whom there is no deceit!" 48Nathanael asked him, "Where did you get to know me?" Jesus answered, "I saw you under the fig tree before Philip called you." 49Nathanael replied, "Rabbi, you are the Son of God! You are the King of Israel!" 50Jesus answered, "Do you believe because I told you that I saw you under the fig tree? You will see greater things than these." ⁵¹*And he said to him, "Very truly, I tell you, you will see heaven opened and the angels of God ascending and descending upon the Son of Man."*

My first Maundy Thursday as a freshly ordained pastor was unremarkable, but my second was, in a word, lit. With the help of a great worship team, we hauled every table in the place to our beautiful but very fixed sanctuary space. Using mountains of black cloth, palms from the previous year's Palm Sunday, cups of juice and various loaves of bread, we curated a scene—a massive table to which everyone was invited, and on to which we were prepared to add as many chairs as needed. It was gorgeous. But it wasn't quite *there*.

I dashed off to the worship closet and grabbed bag after bag of tea lights. We spent the late afternoon dotting the tables with the tiny candles just as the sun was getting ready to set. The image was startlingly beautiful. I was thrilled, and met the wary eye of a comrade in set-up with a smiling, "trust me!" She gently pointed out that kids might not do well around the candles, but my confidence was not to be deterred. The kids could handle it! It would be glorious!

For those keeping track at home, there were approximately thirty-seven seconds between convening this Holy Feast and a brief but robustly terrifying little fire (for the record, it wasn't one of the kids). Humbling, to say the least. Trust me. It'll be fine!

"Trust me" is the big ask at the heart of all churches, all relationships, and all of life. It's what's underneath every pass of the offering plate and every word of the sermon—we are asking you to trust us as stewards of the word. In the denomination in which I was ordained, we place a high value on the many hurdles to ordination as a mark of the trustworthiness of those who make it to the other side. If you can withstand the academic rigor, the years of personal and professional inquiries into your life, the professional training and examinations, then you have a level of earned credibility. This happens because we are asking people to trust us as stewards: keepers and protectors of the holy word, interpreters of the ancient text, and translators of the modern experience into Jesus-friendly terms. We are stewards of secrets. Our roles require confidentiality of us, and we ask a room full of people to listen to us on a weekly basis as we encounter the teachings of God. As parishioners, we are asking clergy and lay-leadership to trust that we will participate with whole hearts and minds, bring the truth with compassion, and be the church to one another and the wider world. There is an unbelievable amount of trust required for this to yield anything like a functional relationship between clergy and parishioners.

Furthermore, this request for trust expands well beyond the sanctuary and applies to all of us. Every time we come into relationship with another, regardless of our church life, we are each of us risking the vulnerability of wondering: Are they worthy of trust? And am I?

Trust on Both Sides of the Pulpit

If I'm honest, becoming a pastor is a bit of an act of trust with limited sight. I am certain there are colleagues out there who have heard The Call, capital T and C, in an unmistakable voice that let them know they were on the right track. I never had that. I had internal conviction, a committed faith, and a robust concept of justice in which I wanted to participate. I love people and wanted to serve them in ways that were compatible with my strengths. I had a gut sense of which passions I pursued were leading in a good direction. I knew joy that seemed from a place beyond myself. But I never knew it as a clarion call from God. "Hey Lyter—get thee to a pulpit!"

Which is why every step of the way, no matter where I've served or worshiped, I felt a mutual sense of asking "trust me" between the church and I. She functions on the trust of all those who participate in her life, and I function in the context of pastor asking for a portion of that trust to be placed in me. And sometimes that trust gets broken, badly. I and every pastor you've ever met knows at least one card-carrying member of the Burned by the Church Wounded Clergy Club. There are certainly days where it seems best to wash the dust off proverbial feet and move away from a system as broken and mean and human as I am.

By now, most young adults (and adults of any age) have a story or two of how they've been hurt, and many of them by the church. We've been disappointed by leaders and felt discouraged by decisions that don't reflect our values. We've watched people who are cruel be given more floor space, voice, and power than those on the fringes.

Even when we lack a personal connection to a faith community, it's hard to miss the broad societal associations with organized religion: the perpetrating and hiding of child sexual abuse, the use of Christ to further political agendas, the church used to shame and banish LGBTQ individuals, using Christ to insist on convictions without nuance regarding women's health and reproductive rights, and so on. It is little wonder that millennials are skeptical. There is the inevitable question that follows: Can anything good come out of organized religion?

So when we are creating a family of choice, many of us prioritize affinity groups over existing institutions. Pub trivia and board game nights with friends over adult education lectures every step of the way. It isn't that we aren't interested in learning or even that we lack a desire to grow spiritually. It's just that the church's sociopolitical mood swings make it darn hard to love her up close.

Mobile Spiritual Homes

Community-building in the millennial world necessitates a quicker build in large part because of our transitory nature. While many of us were raised in rootedness, we have had to build and rebuild families of choice at dozens of locations in our lifetimes. Millennials express hospitality from a place of Judeo-Christian privilege, which means our hospitality doesn't involve the same risk as some of our interfaith siblings, but it remains hospitality nonetheless. Hospitality that expresses a stance far apart from the neutrality in which the hospitality we were raised with exists, but instead, a hospitality that carries with it the sense of urgency and affection that frequent relocation requires. It cuts down on the patience for small talk, to put it mildly.

Finding points of affinity is a tremendous gathering point for millennials and one that doesn't find a natural home in the average church. Affinity is more philosophically profound than just shared interest in flag football or the fact that we happen to like the same books. While those may be fine starting points for organizing people, relationships built on true shared affinity require more emphasis on who you *are* and what you *love* that manifests into your whole being. This is a big, risky ask for vulnerability in sharing those deeper truths and one we church folk just as soon avoid if we can have a chili cook-off instead.

For generations, we have organized people in the church by age and gender above all else. Youth groups, Sunday schools, social events, and retreats often organize along these points of differentiation, taken as given that they will manage to catch and include absolutely everyone. This is no longer sufficient as millennials are more openly accepting of LGBTQIA identities than our predecessors, so we recognize the exclusivity and dismissal that comes with having a "girls group" or a "guys night out." What of the transgender youth or the nonbinary or gender-queer septuagenarian? These boxes are no longer big enough. Maybe they never were, but millennials are making darn sure we see their insufficiency now.

Millennials seek that which I suspect churchgoers of all generations seek: authenticity. And we tend to greet anything less with some amount of suspicion. Fake nice won't cut it, and we're skeptical of institutional capacities for genuine behavior. The speed with which we can know the gory details of a corporate, celebrity, or governmental figure's downfall ensures that we are prepared to be disappointed by practically everyone.

I don't know that Nathanael meant to be so cheeky with his skeptical response: "Can anything good come out of Nazareth?" It's got a hint of that millennial sarcastic droll to it, as if to say: "Honey, I have been to Nazareth and let me tell you, there's nothing worth having coming out of there." But you've got to imagine he had good reason to be skeptical. Here was Philip promising actual, embodied salvation, just up the road, come on and see! Even for men of faith, this is stretching the bounds of friendship in the trust department.

Yet the bond of Nathanael to Philip proved strong enough to get Nathanael in the door, as it were, to open himself up to the possibilities of who Jesus might be. It's no act of blind hope, but rather an act of trusting a friend to lead the way. Of course, once he's there, Nathanael has a whole different set of worries. Nathanael experiences Christ through several transitions. Christ goes from too good to be true to potentially threatening to being a kind of truth that is too profound to be simply labeled "good."

Nathanael asks: How do you know me? Who am I to you and vice versa? He seems to be struggling for position, not understanding the nature of this newfound relationship and seeking familiar ground. The answer is a jarring one: I saw you. I saw you when you first considered whether to come meet me, when you were first invited here. I've seen you all along. I knew your answer before you did and I know you better than you know yourself.

This—the being seen and fully known—is the scaffolding on which affinity connections and lifestyles are built. Not just the surface level of shared interest in gardening or sports, but the more deeply integrated: Who are you? How do you know me? What have I chosen and what will I choose to reveal so that our souls might link a little closer, and what draws us together? Here rests family of choice.

Family of choice does not only mean rejection of one's own family of origin or being rejected by them, though sometimes it can mean either or both. They can be formed as simply as by hosting a Friendsgiving or "orphan Christmas" for those unable to get home for a holiday. The need for extended community is one modernity has attempted to stamp out with the isolation of, and singular focus on, the needs and successes of the nuclear family. Fortunately, in this case, modernity has failed. On some level, we sense that we were called to a more expansive life, and that includes entwining our lives with those of other stages and stories. Births, deaths, and all the key points of life in between demand people who will share in our joy and sorrow. Cultures around the world and, historically, our own, included a broader conception of family, in part to share the celebrations and burdens of life, doubling our joy and halving the weight of the load we carry.

Blood may be thicker than water, but chosen or second families come along when we are fully formed as adults, saving some of the hazards of childhood baggage along the way. Our families of origin will always, on some level, know us for who we were as much if not more than who we are and who we are becoming. This safekeeping of shared memory is good, but can be limiting.

As nomadic as millennials have become, family of choice is a frequent necessity to combat the isolation and loneliness of living in a strange place without the support of loved ones nearby. I'm making it sound as though picking up and moving halfway around the country or the world is easy since millennials do it so often. The truth is that it's heartbreakingly difficult. There are the existential challenges: processing work, relationships, and life with friends over a gap of multiple time zones and feeling like you'll never make friends as good as the ones you left behind and maybe this was all a huge mistake. Missing family-of-origin events—the milestones and the mundane—and knowing that choosing a life anywhere else means choosing a life not there. And then there are the logistics: Where is the grocery store? Did I set up automatic payment correctly? Did I take leave of my senses when I imagined I could handle no in-unit washer and dryer? Is my landlord secretly evil? This is where family of choice comes in, and it isn't an instantaneous connection.

Could the church occupy the space of chosen family for members of the millennial generation? It's possible, but it will not be easy. Letting the church function as a chosen family requires flexibility in our schedules, a less rigid concept of membership, and faster pathways to authentic relationship. We would need to learn to love quickly and hold lightly. We would need to learn to accept people as they are, not as we wish they would be, for it is that level of nonjudgmental acceptance that we tend to seek in our families of choice.

The Church as Family of Choice

In order to join the church, we lay a mountain of work on the applicant, from signing in the "friendship attendance pads," to new member classes, and so on. And joining does not equate to authenticity, of course. It can take years to plug into the life of a community, finding your work and your people within the existing paradigms of the church.

Much more insidious than all these obstacles combined is the church's habit of rejecting non-hetero-patriarchal manifestations of family. We know where to put you if you are single, or married (to the opposite gender identity), or widowed, and that's about it. To build a home that is welcoming and safe to family in all its forms is a great challenge, in part because it requires a more open space and in part because it requires a deeper well of self-knowledge.

A challenge for more openness in who and how we welcome might be a gift. Family of choice depends on the notions of being accepted for who you are and building love where you find it. Churches might foster more of the same by considering carefully how they practice showing love. For a starting point, the institutional church could consider more than just an expansion of the categories into which we put people in an attempt to fit them into our community and meet their needs. We could consider why it is that we feel the need to fit people into certain boxes at all.

Christ calls all kinds to his kin group. When Christ dismisses the notion that his mother and brothers are outside, but insists instead that they are those physically and metaphorically with him on the path of God, he speaks of chosen family. It's not that Jesus suddenly doesn't love his mom or siblings. It is simply that he recognizes a bigger sense of family, one that includes all walks of life and all those who would attempt to walk with him.

Millennials want to know and be known. They want to choose and be chosen into a family in the fullness of their identity. Is the church ready for that?

CHAPTER 7

Ancient Made New: Unbounded Love and Globalism

Acts 4:23-37 (NRSV)

The Believers Pray

²³On their release, Peter and John went back to their own people and reported all that the chief priests and the elders had said to them. ²⁴When they heard this, they raised their voices together in prayer to God. "Sovereign Lord," they said, "you made the heavens and the earth and the sea, and everything in them. ²⁵You spoke by the Holy Spirit through the mouth of your servant, our father David:

"'Why do the nations rage
  and the peoples plot in vain?
²⁶The kings of the earth rise up
  and the rulers band together
against the Lord
  and against his anointed one.'

²⁷Indeed Herod and Pontius Pilate met together with the Gentiles and the people of Israel in this city to conspire against your holy servant Jesus, whom you anointed. ²⁸They did what your power and will had decided beforehand should happen. ²⁹Now, Lord, consider their threats and enable your servants to speak your word with great

Ancient Made New: Unbounded Love and Globalism

> boldness. ³⁰Stretch out your hand to heal and perform signs and wonders through the name of your holy servant Jesus."
>
> ³¹After they prayed, the place where they were meeting was shaken. And they were all filled with the Holy Spirit and spoke the word of God boldly.
>
> ### The Believers Share Their Possessions
>
> ³²All the believers were one in heart and mind. No one claimed that any of their possessions was their own, but they shared everything they had. ³³With great power the apostles continued to testify to the resurrection of the Lord Jesus. And God's grace was so powerfully at work in them all ³⁴that there were no needy persons among them. For from time to time those who owned land or houses sold them, brought the money from the sales ³⁵and put it at the apostles' feet, and it was distributed to anyone who had need.
>
> ³⁶Joseph, a Levite from Cyprus, whom the apostles called Barnabas (which means "son of encouragement"), ³⁷sold a field he owned and brought the money and put it at the apostles' feet.

A well-intentioned but problematic liturgy exists in my tradition. Okay, many of them are well-intentioned but problematic, but my specific concern here surrounds the ways we say goodbye. Here, I refer to the service for recognizing members leaving a church in the PC (USA). This is a service meant to cover a whole host of reasons for departure, and to do so with a sense of ceremony to acknowledge the occasion. In it, those departing are centrally featured at the conclusion of worship. Lay leadership (usually an elder) acknowledges the farewell, the minister reminds us of our baptism, gives thanks for the gifts of the departing members, the congregation collectively chants their thanks for their time together and well-wishes going forward, and a somewhat dry final prayer of peace blesses them on their way.

Let it never be said that the frozen chosen don't know how to party.

There are some good and gracious sentiments in this liturgy and it describes some common feelings around saying goodbye, even if it can't move from description to expression. My issue with this liturgy is twofold: first, it is so stilted in feeling, and second, it does not allow for the possibility that our shared story continues past the moment of farewell.

The departure of a church member is a rupture, and grief over this rupture is expected. And why shouldn't it be? It confirms our care and love for one another, that our time together has mattered, and that this transition away from that physical time together is painful. We should have ways to express such feelings in the life of the church, and failing to acknowledge a departure goes past disrespectful and into the realm of dehumanizing. One of our most hurtful acts as a church can be to ignore it when people leave.

Formalizing a practice and even celebration of goodbye lets us say that which we find hard to articulate, that which so often comes out as anger in the face of separation: I have loved our time together and I am not ready for it to end. There is a real grief in these goodbyes and the frequency of them should not diminish their importance in the life of the church. I am simply suggesting that goodbye is not where we should stop.

There are practical impediments, to be sure, when we attempt to maintain connections with those who have left our pews. We cannot deny the intimacy of being physically present to one another, and Christ is big on showing up. There is a kind of connection that comes from being able to hug someone, a connection that cannot be so easily replaced by Facetime and Snapchat. I cannot envision a healthy community based solely on long-distance interactions. Yet even Jesus was not everywhere that everyone wanted him to be. He took time with just his friends. He took time alone. He wandered and met who he met. And somehow the energy surrounding him did not perish because of these separations. Can we not find the wit and courage to do likewise in our home churches, overcoming the challenge of distance to build pathways toward continued communication for those who have left our community and want to remain connected?

On a theological level, letting goodbye signify the end of a relationship shows remarkably little faith when held up against our professed belief in eternal life. It isn't easy to say goodbye to those we love, whether for a time or for this life entirely. Grappling with mortality is never easy, but if we can't handle an "until we meet again" with some degree of trust, it does give one pause about the depth of our trust in life everlasting. Surely our confidence in God that extends the promise of love literally without end can encourage our love and relationships not to end when someone moves to a new city.

Ancient Made New: Unbounded Love and Globalism

The letters among members of the early church let us know that their fervor and beliefs were just as strong across the miles. Early church relationships had to be held lightly, for who knew how long they would last. New uprisings, jail time, death, distance, disease—any or all could spell the immediate and unceremonious end of a relationship that was foundational to a fledgling faith. There was no room for clinging on too tightly, for just as quickly as the bonds were formed they might be destroyed. The disciples responded to this not by shying away from deep expressions of love, but rather by loving with a quickness of heart and an appreciation for the promises of God. They were ready for goodbye because they held nothing back. To love deeply is, in part, to know that tomorrow is never guaranteed.

Millennials face less on the daily terror front, but their need to have a goodbye at the ready might be just as prevalent. Our father's fathers (and it was, at that point, primarily the fathers who were employed) worked in the same company for their entire careers. We have earned our reputation as job-hoppers. According to Gallup, we identify as *unattached to organizations and institutions* at a rate that far outpaces previous generations. A full 21 percent of us have changed jobs within the past year, and only about half of us say we plan to work at the same place a year from now ("Millennials: the Job-Hopping Generation," Gallup, May 12, 2016). We show consistent openness to new job opportunities and are willing to leap if a new opportunity comes along. As a result, millennials are frequently portrayed as overly fickle or lacking loyalty, though I would contest that by suggesting that instead millennials prioritize being loyal to people and other aspects of our lives. Our generation values our professional identities; we just don't value them the most.

Such a shift in relationships with work represents a monumental cultural swing with far-reaching consequences. There are economic implications of this kind of turnover, and adaptive strategies being undertaken so that companies might benefit from the talents of millennials without being damaged by our changeability. The social implications are also dramatic, as millennials do not put down community roots in the same ways as our predecessors. In fact, the common perspective of churches as such staid institutions may cause religious investment to be a nonstarter for many millennials. If the only way I can fit into this community is by sticking around forever, perhaps it's better to not be involved at all. That would be a real shame, as the interaction between millennials and the institutional church has so very much to gain for all involved. Still, we need to recognize that goodbyes and hellos will be more frequent than ever. Our own institutional receptiveness to change must catch up.

Change to anything can be threatening as all get-out in institutions where we take years to warm up to one another and work overtime to keep our private lives private. The institution of the church as she currently looks is not equipped for frequent mobility and this can translate to love at arms-length, standoffishness that lacks gleeful welcome or warm embrace. We hold off so we don't get hurt. This slowness to incorporate new people into our fold and somewhat stilted expressions of love show up in a thousand tiny ways. The gap between a welcome bag for the stranger, a stick-on name tag, an official printed-just-for-you name tag, and the one you're trusted enough to take home with you stretches for miles.

Our common behaviors in the institutional church tend to communicate love that is unconsciously contingent on staying put. This contingent love is built upon a false promise that anything can, in the grand scheme of things, last. Perhaps all this clinging on to an ideal world that prioritizes stasis of life is a shield, protecting us from the unvarnished view of just how temporary our world and our lives really are. Letting go of that shield and that commitment to stasis may force us to look sharply at our own mortality, but it might just free us up to risk more.

In the face of that view, why not love a bit more recklessly, wherever life happens to find you? Maybe we just need some great encouragers to help us get to the point of being able to love each other like that.

What this Means for the Church

Barnabas, as the relentless cheerleader in the face of some particularly tough crowds, is our starting point. It would be easy to mistake his new moniker of "son of encouragement" as the plaque given for the highest donor at the fundraiser appreciation night, but this encouragement goes deeper than dollars. Barnabas supports from his whole life, including his livelihood. Selling a field is not just an act of tithing, it's a commitment of belief. His confidence in the sufficient provision of this new life was enough that he was willing to release that which kept him fed and functioning up until this point.

Barnabas was never as central a figure as Paul throughout the gospel, yet he's surprisingly mobile and bold. The duo experience more than their fair share of being chased out of towns, discredited, and threatened by those who did not understand and could not believe. To be a source of ongoing encouragement under circumstances such as those is a worthy and brave way to live.

He also functions beautifully as a long-distance cheerleader of the faith journey of others, offering words of support and encouragement in the form of letters and messages sent along where he could not, at the moment, tread. He and Paul worked alike to ensure that their sense of love and support could not be diminished by the miles between themselves and other believers.

Above all, I might be most impressed with the flexibility, energy, and speed of Barnabas. The man does not appear to sit still. Barnabas (originally Joseph from Cyprus), enters the narrative of Christianity by selling a field and giving the proceeds to the disciples, and he later introduces the disciples to Paul himself (Acts 9:27). Barnabas travels back and forth to Antioch, takes multiple trips to Jerusalem, goes back to Cyprus, on to Pamphylia, back again to Antioch, and so forth. Traveling with Silas, Paul, and others, Barnabas was tireless and relentlessly enthusiastic, supportive of the words and works of others and encouraging young churches every step of the way. Barnabas is, or at least could be, a one-man model for the mobility of the church.

Being Barnabas, then, would involve shifting our energies from what could be maintained to what could be created. The church would require a fleetness and facility with shifting identities that are almost completely opposite from where we find ourselves today. As the church, we would emphasize the needs of communities and community members near and far. We would centralize the encouragement of souls over our own comfort. There would be far fewer instances of expecting the world to come to us. We would connect to local communities of faith (all faiths) in meaningful ways and seek to support and encourage their work by developing mutually compassionate relationships. We would show up wherever we were needed. It is a far stretch, but I think Barnabas, a relatively minor character, lives on in the story to help us see a better way to live. I think he survives to remind us just how integral encouragement and support are to the sustenance of faith.

I recognize that we can't all be Barnabas, at least not on an individual level. Some of us are called to motion and some of us are called to be steady. We need all the above to function as the church. The mobility of Barnabas depended upon the hospitality of those he visited. The idea that we would individually become this diasporic movement of would-be disciples in perpetual movement is silly. What I do recommend, though, is that we consider the ways we might be more Barnabas-like as an institution.

There is tremendous value in considering a church on legs, a mobility lost to the steadfastness and security of the local parish. Appreciation for the strengths of mobility becomes a necessary way to think about the world with millennials so often on the move, and homes and families of biology and families of choice scattered across the country and globe. Are millennials being chased down and threatened with bodily harm? Not as such, no. But there is a sense of existentially motivated diaspora that keeps us on the move. Sinking far deeper into the psyche than mere FOMO (Fear Of Missing Out), millennials do seem particularly hungry to soak up the possibilities of life. Granted, privilege dictates the extent to which this can be physically embodied and lived out, but social media presents an opportunity for some equalizing effects: even if I can't be on the other side of the world, my words can instantaneously be anywhere. It is the nature of the viral beast: used for good and for ill, tweets, memes, and ideas themselves can circumnavigate the globe in seconds.

Thus, we see a radical commitment to noncommitment. Not a life uncommitted to anything, but rather less beholden to the trappings of traditional commitments. Buying a house. Staying put. Fixedness. Millennials are not rootless, but rather more like hydroponics, with roots that float in the waters of an unpredictable life, instead of fixed to the certain ground.

Rootlessness and restlessness call for new methods by which to satisfy ubiquitous needs for connection, purpose, and value. The global generation of millennials are not thus just because a lucky few travel the world, but because our exposure to technology at a very young age enables us to connect with global ideas with rapidity and ease. We are immersed in a worldwide pool of pluralism and our constantly-in-transition lives leave us open to genuine consideration of ever more ideas and perspectives.

The benefits of this globalized and unbounded life are that we are becoming keepers of a multiplicity of values, customs, and beliefs, allowing for authentic appreciation of, and connectivity with, those who might previously have been simply "others."

Ancient Made New: Unbounded Love and Globalism

Matthew 25:31-40 (NRSV)

The Judgment of the Nations

> 31 "When the Son of Man comes in his glory, and all the angels with him, then he will sit on the throne of his glory. 32 All the nations will be gathered before him, and he will separate people one from another as a shepherd separates the sheep from the goats, 33 and he will put the sheep at his right hand and the goats at the left. 34 Then the king will say to those at his right hand, 'Come, you that are blessed by my Father, inherit the kingdom prepared for you from the foundation of the world; 35 for I was hungry and you gave me food, I was thirsty and you gave me something to drink, I was a stranger and you welcomed me, 36 I was naked and you gave me clothing, I was sick and you took care of me, I was in prison and you visited me.' 37 Then the righteous will answer him, 'Lord, when was it that we saw you hungry and gave you food, or thirsty and gave you something to drink? 38 And when was it that we saw you a stranger and welcomed you, or naked and gave you clothing? 39 And when was it that we saw you sick or in prison and visited you?' 40 And the king will answer them, 'Truly I tell you, just as you did it to one of the least of these who are members of my family you did it to me.'"

As previously discussed, Christianity calls us to un-other the stranger, and the primary step in that direction is to see and know the stranger so that we might love and serve them. How can we love the unknown? It's counterintuitive to every human instinct for self-protection in the name of survival. The only option is to get to know the unknown and to let people close enough that strangers are just another extension of the family. Education is a key component of this. Since our capacity to know other people is finite, let's joyfully pursue the knowledge and understanding of strangers, especially those we might be most inclined to ignore.

The perils of noncommitment and global pursuits reside in the possibility that we may never land on any one concrete idea or way of being. This isn't just unnerving to members of the preceding generations who love us, it also carries a level of personal existential threat. The line between lifelong explorer and unmoored wanderer is a thin one, and only the person walking the journey can determine if or when that line has been crossed.

Rather than being a signal of flightiness, I believe this signifies millennials as being a new generation characterized by deeply felt embodiment. What we have with us is our bodies, transporting us globally. Ensconced in our bodies is the knowledge that all we have at any moment is this one earthly life. Our bodies carry a peculiar hybrid experience in which our lived experiences are mixed with an inherited and inherent knowledge of the world around us. We know what the world is through our senses, but we also know what the world is through the process of living in it as souls beyond the bounds of our flesh. We interact with the ancients before us and the prophecies ahead of us as a matter of course in our faith (and in many faiths). We carry the truth of wisdom hidden in our daily lives. Therefore, embodiment is becoming where and when we are. Embodiment, ironically enough, gives us a glimpse of the eternal. If the church is here to serve a God unbounded by time, perhaps this millennial perspective on love unbounded by geography can open that timelessness once more.

I hope the institutional church can reframe this noncommitment and globalized lifestyle of so many millennials, seeing instead the awesome possibilities they might model for the church ahead. Can being unbounded by geography give us a window into love bound not by time, location, or anything at all? Yes, and it is my belief that it can help us imagine just a glimpse of the way God loves us, without borders, without limits, without the confines of time.

Becoming Barnabas: Anywhere with Decent Wi-Fi

The simplest way for the church to adapt to this generational reality is to have a more expansive notion of who belongs to the community. Rather than excising one another from roles and from our church life, let us consider how it would be that every one-time participant in the life of this church becomes folded into the forever family, the story of who we are as a family of God. How could we be a better Barnabas—sons and daughters of encouragement—to those whose path takes them away from our own?

Adapting to the concepts of chapter five—that family of choice has a kinship role in the lives of many millennials—is a good start, but the practicalities of the ways this functions in the institutional church will be a challenge. One key aspect of this movement will be to focus mightily on the present and the future, not the past.

Ancient Made New: Unbounded Love and Globalism

We in the church are excellent at memorializing, remembering, and holding on for dear life. This sense of historical worth is central to how we "do church." We centralize where and who we've been. Think about it. A time of remembrance? Absolutely normal. A time for possibility? What would that even mean?

If we could somehow balance our sense that all is both impermanence and eternal love above all else, we might get close to understanding how to make the ancient new again. This is a holy, mighty task, and a big human challenge, that we might find words and ways of loving well while holding one another lightly. It will not do to love at arm's length, protecting ourselves from the pain of eventual and inevitable loss. Nor will it do to hold so tightly that our love becomes like suffocation, stifling us into behaviors that diminish the fullness of life others might live. It will only do to find a way to live into this duality, dismissing the urge to live in a binary world of separation from one extreme to the other, instead embracing the simultaneity of both.

This might prove an extraordinary challenge in times as anxious as these. Globalization refers to a multiplicity of experiences and influences. It refers to the diasporic and perpetual movement of millennials, as previously used in this text. That energy in motion rides on the back of technology, but also the social and political processes that connect us globally. It does not arrive without consequences. The latter carries extraordinary baggage as the negative aspect of this same globalizing coin. While the connection we gain through shared ideas and experiences can be salvific, the burdens placed on some nations far exceed the benefits. Those in the global south in particular have experienced violence, economic deprivation, and increased vulnerability through many iterations of globalization and I would be remiss if I didn't acknowledge that wounding.

Globalization in the neoliberal, sociopolitical, and financial sense has amped our collective anxiety to an eleven. Not only do we know the moment a disaster strikes on the other side of the world and find ourselves confronting the real-time footage of shocking pain and loss, we share the knowledge that our inextricability often leads to that very suffering. Our choices in how we care for or, more accurately, fail to care for our planet, cause the anxious confrontation that our dependence on our cars leads to climate refugees, famines, and deaths in more impoverished parts of the world. Our choices in how much or how little we are willing to pay for our clothes determines the sustenance of organizations that thrive on child and slave labor. We cannot pretend we have ignorance of these insidious ways in which we are connected and globalization calls us to reckon with the disconnect of our choices and our ideals.

Anxiety locks us into a kind of tennis match, snapping our eyes from future fears unrealized to memories of what's been lost or at least what has been perceived to be lost, leaving no space to breathe, be, and hold the moment. If the church could allow herself a season, or even a day, of no anticipation and no lurking in the past, what would we even talk about?

Consider instead positioning ourselves fully in the present. Where are we on this day? Where is God in this moment? It could be a great exercise in practical theology to ask all participants to notice how much of worship is spent in the past and in the future, and how very little is spent in the present moment. Millennials' inclination toward the immediate, accentuated by FOMO, can be a helpful guide here as we consider that all we have and all we are is transitory at best. The application of this philosophy toward the experiences of a faith community could be a bit earth-shattering, particularly if we were to consider the worship hour as more than just a spiritual feeding session. If we considered, at least on occasion, how that hour might look if we knew it was the last one we'd ever have, I think we'd get close to the kind of radical presence the original disciples were embodying.

Maybe from there we can unlock our anxiety cages that keep us from freely imagining and expressing ourselves. Such freedom might free us from inhibitions, granting a sense of the future possible instead of the future feared long enough to see it well.

A Liturgy of Possibility

For what we can imagine together, and the unimaginable, we pray.

For the hellos that have not yet occurred, the doors not yet created, let alone flung open as invitation, we pray.

For that which we have not yet dared to consider, we pray.

For those we don't know how to invite in, those new members of our family whose existence is not yet known to us, we pray.

For those among us with unknown gifts, and the unknown futures awaiting each of us, we pray.

For all that is made possible, through you O God, we pray.

CHAPTER 8

Instagram Faith: Crucifixion Instantaneous

Matthew 10:5-23 (NRSV)

The Mission of the Twelve

5 These twelve Jesus sent out with the following instructions: "Go nowhere among the Gentiles, and enter no town of the Samaritans, 6 but go rather to the lost sheep of the house of Israel. 7 As you go, proclaim the good news, 'The kingdom of heaven has come near.' 8 Cure the sick, raise the dead, cleanse the lepers, cast out demons. You received without payment; give without payment. 9 Take no gold, or silver, or copper in your belts, 10 no bag for your journey, or two tunics, or sandals, or a staff; for laborers deserve their food. 11 Whatever town or village you enter, find out who in it is worthy, and stay there until you leave. 12 As you enter the house, greet it. 13 If the house is worthy, let your peace come upon it; but if it is not worthy, let your peace return to you. 14 If anyone will not welcome you or listen to your words, shake off the dust from your feet as you leave that house or town. 15 Truly I tell you, it will be more tolerable for the land of Sodom and Gomorrah on the day of judgment than for that town.

Coming Persecutions

16 "See, I am sending you out like sheep into the midst of wolves; so be wise as serpents and innocent as doves. 17 Beware of them, for they will hand you over to councils and flog you in their synagogues; 18 and you will be dragged before governors and kings because of me, as a testimony to them and the Gentiles. 19 When they hand you over, do not worry about how you are to speak or what you are to say; for what you are to say will be given to you at that time; 20 for it is not you who speak, but the Spirit of your Father speaking through you. 21 Brother will betray brother to death, and a father his child, and children will rise against parents and have them put to death; 22 and you will be hated by all because of my name. But the one who endures to the end will be saved. 23 When they persecute you in one town, flee to the next; for truly I tell you, you will not have gone through all the towns of Israel before the Son of Man comes.

Christ's sales pitch to followers could use a little re-branding, a marketing brush-up if you will. It worked because of the source, but it would be incredibly difficult to convince a lot of modern-day would-be disciples to follow this path. Let's try it again, shall we?

"If you're going my way, you'll see the world! Meet new people! Gain a sense of moral superiority while traveling so light you'll think you invented eco-friendly travel two millennia early! Participate in ancient customs to really appreciate the new cultures you'll encounter along the way while making a *real* difference. This job has its tough moments, but I guarantee you'll have the time of your life, even when you're fleeing for your life! We want *you* to carry that good, good news for big dividends at journey's end!"

Okay, it might be a little misleading, and it most certainly would have attracted an alternative crowd. And in today's entertainment-obsessed culture striving always for distinction, it might just work. But it would be, of course, a total betrayal because Christ is eminently real about the fact that suffering is going to come for all those who follow his path. And we, the church of today, do *not* like to suffer.

When Fear Takes Us Down

Once, very early in my tenure as a preacher, a man wandered in during a worship service. He appeared to be inebriated, unkempt and weaving, meandering down the center aisle toward the table behind which I stood for prayers. His mumblings were incoherent, but included a wide variety of colorful epithets directed at a generic "you"; it was unclear as to whether God, the congregation, I, or none of the above were the targets of his invectives. He wandered back out moments later, and we included prayers for those who might be feeling lost. It was a slightly harrowing moment in a small church where this sort of thing very rarely happens. The experiences I and my peers in urban ministry have had elsewhere would refer to this as "Tuesday." But there and then, it produced a tangible sense of fear among the community.

Of course, it was just one moment, forgettable enough in a string of Sundays. The moment itself wasn't so very big at all. It was the aftermath that was so striking. At the lightning-quick speed of gossip at which churches excel, factions were formed. The congregation self-divided into five key groups: it's no big deal (for some), what if he had turned violent (a fair question), we need to train the ushers to handle this sort of thing (okay), we should call the police (nope), we need to lock the doors during worship (absolutely not). To the last, I made the kind of passionate, perhaps arrogant declaration that comes with youth: try it, and I'll preach from the front steps outside. What was palpable in the aftermath of this one small moment was the hair-trigger response to fear in the life of this community. As their preacher, I had to contend with this fear. What was its source? What maintained it or kept it at bay? Where was my complicity in blocking God's clarion call to "fear not?"

This microcosm of fear in the church is no indictment of this particular community or this particular moment: all of their feelings and my own were founded in our individual reads on the situation. The degree to which we experienced or anticipated violence was a real, if partial view of this situation. What it does indicate is the degree to which we give the concept of picking up our cross a fair bit of lip service. What if the cross comes through the door looking for you?

Fear has its place in life and in the church. Scripture doesn't suggest that even Christ was fearless. Certainly, it does not suggest that he approached his crucifixion unafraid. In fact, quite the opposite.

Luke 22:39–44 (NRSV)

He came out and went, as was his custom, to the Mount of Olives; and the disciples followed him. **40***When he reached the place, he said to*

> them, "Pray that you may not come into the time of trial." **41** Then he withdrew from them about a stone's throw, knelt down, and prayed, **42** "Father, if you are willing, remove this cup from me; yet, not my will but yours be done." **43** Then an angel from heaven appeared to him and gave him strength. **44** In his anguish he prayed more earnestly, and his sweat became like great drops of blood falling down on the ground.

Christ is, in a word, terrified of what is to come. How could he be otherwise? Degrees of divinity all set aside, crucifixion is a horrifying way to die, deliberately as painful and humiliating as possible. There's a reason the Romans used this as punishment for slaves, enemies of the state, or insurrectionists. Christ is begging for his life while maintaining a steadfast gaze on God's will being done. He's withdrawn so he is alone. He prays with such fervor that an angel appears to bolster his nerve, but even that is not enough to save him from a feeling of "anguish." It's unthinkable that he would be anything other than deeply afraid. And the angel giving him strength is both an acknowledgment and assuagement of that palpable fear. His willingness to go where God leads is not a disavowal of the fear Christ feels on the path. There is something oddly comforting about the notion that Christ experiences fear. It means he is so deep in his humanity that he is relatable, for there is no one among us who wouldn't reflect such terror.

Fear exists for Christ, and it is here for us, and it is valid. It's an undeniable part of the lived human experience. It cannot be ignored, but it also cannot be the center of our world, and particularly the world of the church wherein we champion a God who tells followers over and over again: Fear not! It cannot be fear that is the deciding factor in who we are or what we do, in our behavior or in our character.

Love in a Dangerous Time

On the recent memory of a white supremacist preying on the hospitality of a prayer group in Mother Emanuel AME Church in Charleston, South Carolina, we cannot dismiss the reality that lives are cut short in hateful, sudden ways. Twelve people were shot, nine died, and it rode on the backs of racism and hatred stoked in the mind of one white domestic terrorist. It was a shocking and horrific event, made all the more tragic by the fact that mass shootings have become frequent and nearly common in the American experience. In 2016, a man killed forty-nine people and wounded fifty-eight others in Pulse, a gay nightclub in Orlando, Florida. Both hate crimes, both robbing life as well as a sense of safety in a place that is meant to be sacred and that draws together those seeking a common life. Both forever altering those communities. Both used to express hatred through violence and fear. Both acts of supreme cowardice, attempting to rupture love in its various forms.

Just because I have never had my personal safety threatened in a church setting doesn't mean I would even consider advocating that congregations are required to invite the violent into their midst, or aren't wise to consider how to keep those in the space safe. Those murdered were not sacrificial lambs on some altar of love. They were victims of hate-fueled, blind, and senseless violence. The slaying of those church members is abhorrent, tragic, and cruel. Given the gun culture of the US, church members are wise to engage with the practicalities of danger invading this sacred space. It can be murky waters indeed to separate out the needs of defending in a violent reality and the plaintive insistence of fear. As we live in a world where violence on the whole has gradually decreased, it is worth paying attention to the facts versus the perception when it comes to fear. Careful discernment is required and none of us is in a position to call others to sacrifice their own safety for the maintenance of an ideal.

On a practical level, we are asked to maintain a healthy relationship with an often-irrational emotion: fear. We are called by those who come to us for sanctuary and solace to balance fear that is reflective of actual reality with faith that moves with, through, and beyond fear and to do so in a practical way. This is not an easy or enviable place to be. We can make certain assumptions based on relative crime rates, knowledge of our neighbors and local needs, trends in hate crimes, and so forth; however, we are required to decide whether we lock the church up like a fortress in the name of keeping what's inside safe, or leaving the place open and risking the unknown that can come inside. These are practical decisions to be made by the individuals who occupy each community, and while I caution against motivation by blind fear, they are not decisions anyone else can make for you. It is between your community and God.

Golgotha Awaits

Beyond the practicalities of balancing safety and fear, though, there remains the theological underpinnings of decisions we make. What drives us, if not our fear? In faith, we are driven by hope. We are a community built on the empty cross. The empty cross is not a cross that forgets. It stands firm as if to say oh yes, he was here; the fear and pain are absolutely real, but he is here no longer. He has moved on and the empty cross leads to the empty tomb, subverting our fear by posing the impossible: that death could not contain him.

As an underlying motivation, the empty cross should impact our response to the call that we pick up our own cross and follow him. Congregations would be well challenged to consider what it means to shoulder the instrument of our own death and follow this man to the (our) end. Is the cross we bear self-imposed or drama-fueled, the kinds of irritations bordering on frivolity that we can point to as our suffering? Our personal cross is a calling to bear a portion of the world's need, and it is difficult to locate that in an authentic way from the relative safety and privilege of the ordinary pew, which reveals our general embarrassment of riches. Not that our people don't suffer—they do, in all the ordinary ways that life brings suffering. The death of a loved one, illness in a child, a dissolving relationship, professional loss, health challenges: all of these are forms of very real and tangible suffering, I'm just not convinced they are what Christ was referring to when he called us to come along.

The cross isn't ordinary suffering. It is the sacrifice of humanity, dignity, and life itself for the sake of something much, much bigger. The cross implicates all of humanity in reminding us of the ways in which we hurt each other, particularly the vulnerable among us. It convicts the self and it convicts the species. It is tempting to think that Christ went to the cross that we might not have to suffer, but he explicitly calls us to pick up a cross and follow him.

If and when we could find a cross to carry, I imagine we'd do so with great trepidation. Be very wary of an enthusiastic cross-carrier, because I'm not convinced the world needs more martyrs. I think the world needs people with their eyes open and a willingness to do what needs to be done not for the glory but for the simple fact that it needs to be done. We do so without hope in earthly resurrection. We do so without a path to escape from the pain along the way. We do so because it is such a way that he calls us.

As a community, there might be no good way for us to confront the real and instant reality of the cross. We tend to want to keep the cross at a distance—as jewelry or art piece—without confronting the ways in which we are all of us called to follow into unknown territories, to lead into communities that do not want to meet Christ, to persecution, and even to death.

There is a peculiar and particular darkness to the centrality of the historically fixed crucifixion story in Christian identity. Jesus was hardly the only person crucified—not by a long shot. Nor was he the sole falsely accused soul sentenced to execution: not the first, and not the last by centuries. And yet the story persists and I have a hunch it would regardless of the resurrection aftermath. The story of Christ's path to the cross is as impactful as his departure from it. We are driven by and toward this sacrificial moment in the story, this alignment with the poorest and most vulnerable among us. From his birth onward, his death is foretold, from the balms for death brought as gifts for the newborn king to the near end when he allows a woman to cleanse his feet with expensive perfume and her hair. As fond as I am personally of an emphasis on the birth and life of Christ, the pall of death is an inescapable and functional part of the story.

The omnipresence of death might be because the moment of crucifixion is an encapsulating globe—a moment of full-depth human experience, preserved, timeless. It is simultaneously imbibed and created, a Mobius strip of the worst and best of what we can be. We fixate: we can't look away and we don't want to. Christ knows this about us as is evidenced by his warnings and entreaties to his disciples. He knows that, deep down, we want to be led toward that which is worth living for and worth dying for, even if it means looking true horror in the eye along the way. On some level, we've been doing just that all along.

Creatio ex Everything

The Instagrammed life is not so different from the ongoing obsession with the crucifixion as we might imagine. It may serve as silly distraction to perpetually document a curated version of our lives and observe the curated versions of others' lives, but it may also serve as a point of access to the kinds of agony and ecstasy that humans are perpetually inclined to seek; a mobile and miniature version of the arc of drama that forever seeks that which evokes the strongest emotions.

Instagram is just one such access point for that and a release valve for those inclinations. Just as we can keep up with the antics of our friends' pets and toddlers, so too come the live feeds of cruelty crisscrossing the world. We get the best, the silliest, the weirdest, and the worst of humanity in an unfettered barrage of data, and we are left to try to make sense of it all. It allows us to distance ourselves while imbibing previously unimaginable quantities of data, perhaps dulling pain through frequent but remote exposure.

God may have created the world *ex nihilo* (out of nothing), but the Instagram generation therefore is attempting to do the next-to-impossible—creation ex everything. I'm sure the continual advancement in technology will prove this idea laughably cute in a decade or so, as the whole wealth of knowledge continues to grow exponentially. What feels like drinking from a firehose today will be a veritable water fountain compared to what is coming next, which will surely be an amplified version of everything.

That said, our world today requires nothing less than the co-construction of meaning and truth based on a tsunami of information, particularly when living with and counteracting a culture of fear. Critical thought is an essential skill for survival. Creation, consumption, and discernment, all simultaneously enacted, are the perpetual work of those connected by social media. It is in and through social media that so much fiction and a little reality are funneled. It is up to the participant to seek out and create their own understanding of the truth along the way. Weeding out the fears that are worth having from the fears that are meant to manipulate us is a skill-set that is becoming more important by the day.

Mark 3:1–19 (NRSV)

The Man with a Withered Hand

> *Again he entered the synagogue, and a man was there who had a withered hand.* 2*They watched him to see whether he would cure him on the sabbath, so that they might accuse him.* 3*And he said to the man who had the withered hand, "Come forward."* 4*Then he said to them, "Is it lawful to do good or to do harm on the sabbath, to save life or to kill?" But they were silent.* 5*He looked around at them with anger; he was grieved at their hardness of heart and said to the man, "Stretch out your hand." He stretched it out, and his hand was restored.* 6*The Pharisees went out and immediately conspired with the Herodians against him, how to destroy him.*

Instagram Faith: Crucifixion Instantaneous

A Multitude at the Seaside

>7Jesus departed with his disciples to the sea, and a great multitude from Galilee followed him; 8hearing all that he was doing, they came to him in great numbers from Judea, Jerusalem, Idumea, beyond the Jordan, and the region around Tyre and Sidon. 9He told his disciples to have a boat ready for him because of the crowd, so that they would not crush him; 10for he had cured many, so that all who had diseases pressed upon him to touch him. 11Whenever the unclean spirits saw him, they fell down before him and shouted, "You are the Son of God!" 12But he sternly ordered them not to make him known.

Jesus Appoints the Twelve

>13He went up the mountain and called to him those whom he wanted, and they came to him. 14And he appointed twelve, whom he also named apostles to be with him, and to be sent out to proclaim the message, 15and to have authority to cast out demons. 16So he appointed the twelve: Simon (to whom he gave the name Peter); 17James son of Zebedee and John the brother of James (to whom he gave the name Boanerges, that is, Sons of Thunder); 18and Andrew, and Philip, and Bartholomew, and Matthew, and Thomas, and James son of Alphaeus, and Thaddaeus, and Simon the Cananaean, 19and Judas Iscariot, who betrayed him.

Jesus and his disciples alongside him are creating out of both an old world and a new one: old in which the existing religious structures have a tight grip on declaring what is permissible and what is punishable, and a new one in which miraculous healing has become possible. This new world was revelation in process, both to those who wanted it so desperately they practically drowned Jesus for it, and those who feared it and longed to shut it down. The powers that be were in no hurry to acquiesce their power, nor did they implicitly trust this young guy from Nazareth who was upsetting the balance. And no one could know quite what to expect or how to create, move, or be in the world Christ was shaping through the surrounding haze of fear culture. It was a new world and it wasn't done being formed yet.

Vagabonding

Growing Up in a World Falling Apart

Dancing on the outer limits of millennial-dom as I write this (thirty-three years old in 2017), I see our unique space in the world. We came of age with the internet. We have only dim memories of a world before instantaneous global communication was possible. We remember the nightly news, but few of us use it for our main source of information now. Many of us were in the heart of our formative years when two key events to US culture and identity occurred: the Columbine shootings in 1999, and September 11, 2001. In these events, a new world was created. We had known violence as a culture before, of course we had. We've been perpetrating violence on whole civilizations since the US first began, and experiencing it within our own constructs all along. These events, however, stand out as markers of lost innocence for the millennial generation as the former impacted our peer group directly, while the latter occurred in our key formative years of adolescence, and both were broadcast in such a way as to shift the way our worlds would work.

In Columbine, we learned our safe places were not safe. This wasn't the first instance of school violence and, most tragically, nowhere near the last. But it did introduce us to a whole new vernacular: armed intruder drills, lockdown drills, and discussions about how best to secure an elementary school classroom. We learned that school was as dangerous as any place else, and that violence of this kind of focused and life-ending hatred could make anyone a target at any time. Those of us in school at the time imagined what it would mean to have to hide from an intruder, for our cafeteria or library to become a site of war-like violence, minus the war itself.

And on September 11, 2001, we learned that America was not invulnerable, at once ruptured in a particularly violent and horrifying manner. We watched as the second tower was hit, and as it fell, we had no one to interpret for us what this meant or what was coming next. The world did not think us perfect. It thought of us as a giant in need of felling. The years of resulting war would teach us that America was not infallible either. Our world became an insecure place where international violence was as possible as domestic (a reality many other nations live with on a daily basis but of which we in the US were largely ignorant), and our experiences of airports, militarized police, international wars, and privacy would be forever shaped by the events of that day.

So as the church attempts to integrate the lives of millennials, it might be best to consider the ways their church, their country, and their world

Instagram Faith: Crucifixion Instantaneous

remain places of insecurity. There is an impact from growing up knowing that every trip to the airport meant removing our shoes, carrying only a certain number of ounces of toothpaste, and a sense of personal invasion.; coming to understand that the one group of people you were always supposed to ask for help if you were white were actually the bearers of deepest terror and harm to our siblings of color; growing up mistrusting a government after the revelation of lie after lie that led to war after war, both domestic and far away. It is a deeply insecure world and it is surprising that insecurity doesn't translate more directly to nonparticipatory cynicism, a generation of apathetic hostility. Yet it doesn't. We engage, we connect, and we try to learn in spite of feeling insecure and overwhelmed by it all.

As a result, we may be quick to love and yet slow to trust, urgent with passion and hesitant to join, broadly connected and yet unsure of the depths we can swim before we drown. Ignoring these facets of the millennial experience will only cause further distance between the generations and dearly held systems. The institutional church must recognize this, must see these dimensions of millennial life, and must be patient with them.

Our brains and society have not had time to catch up with the speed and blunt force of instantaneous news. Social media connects, but also presents the potential existential crisis of real-time violence. Videos that play automatically now populate our social media feeds, and that includes current events with violence in real time. We shouldn't look away from the world's pain and suffering, but the lack of choice, time, or space in imbibing this information is overpowering.

The phenomenon of real-time violence isn't entirely new. I recall watching the OJ Simpson car chase with my family, and my parents shushing me up the stairs, indicating "we don't know how this is going to end." That phrase persists with me as a deep truth—we don't know how this is going to end, and yet now it isn't so simple as turning off the TV. The second we scroll, the videos start without prompting, the information is there, there, there—closer than an arm's length away. In our hands, in our minds, in an instant.

All of this comes into sharp relief against the increasingly brazen forces of empire. The divisiveness of political polemic may never have been quite so abject in the US as in the 2016 election cycle and its aftermath. We don't just disagree with each other, we now operate in realms of the appalling, in the spaces of true hatred. Our divisions have ceased even feigning to be about achieving a greater good. Instead, defensiveness and acrimony have become acceptable forms of public discourse. Our empire is doing as empires before us have: destroying itself under the weight of its own ceaseless consumption, self-aggrandizement, and indifference to the needs of humanity, particularly our most vulnerable citizens.

Let's be clear, empire has been here since well before Christ and perhaps it always will. But an empire based on cisgender, hetero, patriarchal, white supremacy cannot withstand the daily demolitions of the millions of voices against it, and those millions of voices are amplified by social media. We see more, so we know more, we speak more and so we are compelled to attempt to do more. We are critical and aware of the fact that a large swath of our culture is wrapped up in maintaining fear, and that aspect of the empire must fall. It will involve looking straight into the onslaught of information, misleading statistics, and cherry-picked stories with great financial investment in keeping fear alive. And only by moving through that fear in the search for critical, collaboratively conceptualized truth can we be rid of it. But how might that be done?

One reasonable response to all this might be to take no bag with you. To travel light, for there's no way of knowing what tomorrow will bring. Jesus asks his followers near the very end of his life: "When I sent you without purse, bag or sandals, did you lack anything?" "Nothing," they answered (Luke 22:35). It's almost as if this Jesus fellow was on to something. The mechanics of traveling without a bag in the life of the church are worth pondering. What baggage do we carry in the life of the church? What do we store (and hoard) in the name of preparation for a rainy day? What do we lock up because we are afraid of something happening to it, and what might happen to us as a result? Every community has their version of the precious treasures, and usually they signify no small amount of emotional baggage along with them. How might we consider life without these extra purses full of supplies, physically or spiritually?

Rather than a life on the run, consider that this might be an invitation to a life of selective attachments. It is limiting our attachment to things and places, not to people. It is not a matter of detaching or an attempt to live a life free of the painful consequences of commitment, relationship, or geographic stability. Rather, it is sensing the diffuse and widespread possibilities of love under the boot of empire.

CHAPTER 9

Beloved Disciples and Authenticity of Faith

John 19:16–30 (NRSV)

The Crucifixion of Jesus

So they took Jesus; **17***and carrying the cross by himself, he went out to what is called The Place of the Skull, which in Hebrew is called Golgotha.* **18***There they crucified him, and with him two others, one on either side, with Jesus between them.* **19***Pilate also had an inscription written and put on the cross. It read, "Jesus of Nazareth, the King of the Jews."* **20***Many of the Jews read this inscription, because the place where Jesus was crucified was near the city; and it was written in Hebrew, in Latin, and in Greek.* **21***Then the chief priests of the Jews said to Pilate, "Do not write, 'The King of the Jews,' but, 'This man said, I am King of the Jews.'"* **22***Pilate answered, "What I have written I have written."* **23***When the soldiers had crucified Jesus, they took his clothes and divided them into four parts, one for each soldier. They also took his tunic; now the tunic was seamless, woven in one piece from the top.* **24***So they said to one another, "Let us not tear it, but cast lots for it to see who will get it." This was to fulfill what the Scripture says,*

"They divided my clothes among themselves,
 and for my clothing they cast lots."

> ²⁵*And that is what the soldiers did.*
>
> *Meanwhile, standing near the cross of Jesus were his mother, and his mother's sister, Mary the wife of Clopas, and Mary Magdalene.* ²⁶*When Jesus saw his mother and the disciple whom he loved standing beside her, he said to his mother, "Woman, here is your son."* ²⁷*Then he said to the disciple, "Here is your mother." And from that hour the disciple took her into his own home.*
>
> ²⁸*After this, when Jesus knew that all was now finished, he said (in order to fulfill the Scripture), "I am thirsty."* ²⁹*A jar full of sour wine was standing there. So they put a sponge full of the wine on a branch of hyssop and held it to his mouth.* ³⁰*When Jesus had received the wine, he said, "It is finished." Then he bowed his head and gave up his spirit.*

At the very end of this and every story we tell, we must look at who stays, who speaks, and who acts. Whether these are stories acted out through new technologies or stories inherited through families or stories passed by oral tradition centuries ago, they are our primary way of constructing the world around us. Our stories comprise us, building our shared reality, and without our stories, we are nothing.

To begin, who stays: the women. Of course, the women. The Marys three, loyal in the face of excruciating loss they were powerless to stop. It is unthinkable to watch such a thing happen to anyone at all, let alone one so loved. Yet there the women stayed. The Bible isn't big on character development, particularly where women are concerned, so we can only guess as to their thoughts and feelings throughout this ordeal. These women, made insignificant by their gender, can keep close watch without necessarily incurring Roman wrath, though there is no guarantee of safety here or anywhere. Their helplessness to alleviate or end Christ's suffering is palpable. Yet they show up—demonstrating the authenticity of love.

Were they afraid? Appalled? Terrified? Yes, undoubtedly. It wouldn't matter if they'd seen this done to others, this was their Jesus—their rabbi, friend, and son.

It is tempting to view these characters as an opportunity for us, allowing the remote readers in periods separated by centuries to relate to the unimaginable by connecting our own lives as parents, children, friends with this incredible loss. The problem with this is that it tends, so often, to be emotionally manipulative, which is especially cheap when used in preaching. When our hearts get tugged at by a stirring rendition of "Mary Did You Know" (my vote for Best Summary of How Mansplaining Works in a Song), we are denying these Marys their own personhood and experience by supplanting it with how it impacts us. We compare them to how we think we would feel in the same position.

Tempting though such comparisons might be, I find it problematic for the same reasons as the anti-rape campaigns insisting that "she's somebody's daughter, sister, mother, friend, wife, aunt, niece, etc." would be primary reasons that one should oppose rape culture, as if one's position and relationship to others (particularly men) determine the entirety of a woman's character or why she shouldn't be raped. Using the three Marys as an entryway to the pain of Christ's death feels similarly cheap. As someone wise suggested, let's cross out everything after "she's somebody." She is a fully valued human being regardless of her relationship to others. So it could be for Mary, Mary, and Mary.

In addition to careful thought about who was there and who was absent, the text calls us to consider what was spoken. One can easily imagine the need for brevity so close to Christ's final breaths, and his choice to ensure the mutual care of his mother and his beloved disciple is telling. As you have belonged to me and I to you, now you belong to one another. The last gasps of breath squeezed out by a grasping, cruel empire, and it all comes down to something so much smaller and so much more sacred than grand sweeping statements. It comes down to making sure love is spoken and clear. By calling for the mutual love and care of this mother and beloved disciple, he isn't just stating his final will, but planting the seeds that his love must be carried onward in the lives of those whom he loves.

If the church were about to breathe her last, I wonder what database systems would be most important to preserve or which bulletin templates would call forth our great passion to protect. Considering what we'd try to save in the end has a way of sharpening the senses and shedding clear light on what we value. Who or what would your church find most precious in the end? What could we lose that would truly diminish our identity as Christians? Really, I think if we were truly confronted with our own mortality as an institution (or as individuals), we would be quicker to recognize that the survival of self is nothing when compared to the survival of the central thesis of it all: love.

Eternal in Temporary Times

Love is the sacred, eternal, ancestral, and prophetic tie that binds across all our differences and generational gaps. Love becomes mistaken for a lot of common experiences: affection, affinity, general accord and agreement. Let us not confuse our Very Nice Ideas, polite habits, and twee belief in tiny chubby baby angels with that wall-breaking, empire-destroying love modeled by Jesus Christ. Know then, when I say love, I mean the latter. This is love that marks the distinction between feeling good and being good, between telling someone what they want to hear or what will be easy to say as opposed to telling them the truth. It isn't *carte blanche* to be cruel and call it compassion, but rather an insistence that love speaks truthfully and does not back down from power. This is the core of the nature of Christ.

Central to the church's roots and base identity, Christ calls us to shed our insecure obsession with self-presentation, all in the name of love. None of this can be about looking good, and for all that is good and holy let us resist the attempt to look cool. There is nothing cool about what we profess to believe in, and if we follow Christ with all that we have and are, life is going to be the antithesis of easy. On some level, I think most churches know this, but we still fall into the frequent trap of attempting to hook the youngsters by attempting to make the ancient hip.

If I could remove any single word from the vernacular of church life, it would be "relevant" (with "emergent" as a close second). Relevant is even now a bit dated as a buzzword of the early 1990s, the consideration of what was popular in culture, language, and style that might connect generations and hook in the younger crowds. It is, to say the least, off-putting. It has been overused practically to the point of meaninglessness, and most generally refers to those instances in which, like Cinderella's step-sisters and the glass slipper, the church tries to force itself into the wrong shape for the sake of becoming what it shouldn't attempt to be in the first place.

First and foremost, it's unbelievably condescending. It dumbs down the gospel, presuming a new generation lacks the attention span or the capacity for delayed gratification. It infers an endless drive to be entertained on the part of the young. Millennials actually have a profound appreciation for the timeless, as evidenced by the resurgence of ancient liturgical practices making the rounds. Even more profoundly, the same core ideas still have the broadest appeal: to hear and be heard, to grow within and alongside a community, to love and be loved well.

Secondly, attempts to be relevant are frequently poorly executed. I'm all for experimenting in worship and joyfully embrace the fact that experiments often fail. It is the way we learn and grow. We can attempt the playful and even silly, and there is something glorious about attempting to find meaningful ways to draw connections between the pews and the sublime. The key word here being *meaningful*. Worship that is imitative and reductive for the sake of being entertaining is at high risk for being less than meaningful, and doubly so when it is poorly executed for the sake of vanity exercises. If we who are designing and leading worship play too much for laughs, for chumminess, for easy tears, for shoehorning in catchy songs, then we imperil the authenticity of the moment. We make it about us, not God. Too often, the church experiments without attending to the real results, responding to whims over participating in genuine acts of worship.

And thirdly, perhaps above all, this capriciousness in church life makes a trend of the timeless, a fashion out of the unfathomable that is eternity. By latching on to every nearest trend, we lose sight of the fact that much of what we do has ancient roots. Instead of drawing out those connections with our parishioners of any age and displaying confidence in their capacity to participate in the ancient-made-new, we pander as though their attention cannot be kept. Why are we trying so hard to be keyed in to the singular moment of today when we are called to stand amidst that which is eternal?

This isn't anything new—churches try to reinvent themselves within the walls of their own traditions for each new generation. We do it to save ourselves, knowing that new life is essential to our survival. A litany of traditions past: for the house churches and cake walks, Jesus seminars and weekend retreats, preaching without notes and three-points-and-a-poem homiletics, and the additions of millennials themselves. I'm as culpable as the next millennial clergy, having led a twist on the popular Beer and Hymns gatherings with Vermouth and Vespers (we had a friend who owned a local martini bar), where twenty- and thirty-somethings would gather to discuss theology and life. It was irritatingly hipster of us, but it was fun. We adapt; we try new things. No shame in that as long as it isn't just a mad grab for easy trends. As long as it's a conscious effort to focus ever closer on the roots of it all: Christ's love.

While we're considering ways to keep the eternal central to our church experience, we ought to address the way we tend to interact with millennials who are new to our communities. We've got a bad habit of swarming newcomers under age forty and sighing heavily if they don't know (or care about) the unwritten codified rules of *our* church home by the third week, or if they don't come back at all. Like vampires hungry for fresh blood, we betray our own insecurities of who we are as we currently exist for the sake of who we might become, or who we think we might become with just enough young (heteronormative, married, etc.) families in our pews. We so desperately want people to come in and join and stay that we fail to recognize who they actually are in the process.

Music is great; it's hard to fathom church without it. That said, simply adding a band won't do it. Music, like preaching, liturgy, and all the trappings of worship, is meant to facilitate our connection with God. These things are not the connection itself. Worship is what happens in and between the hearts of a community and their God. Thinking a praise band is the path to that end is a bit preposterous, just like assuming a well-preached sermon is the missing link between us and the Almighty.

Social media is a helpful communication tool, but it's just a tool, as was the website before it, and the newsletter before that. Facebook, Twitter, Instagram, Snapchat: none of these modalities will change what lies at the core of your community. Use them well if you're going to use them at all, and don't imagine for a moment that those who are thirty-five and under will flock because you tweeted. Substance has most assuredly not gone out of style.

I sense the irony in preaching about the value of eschewing trendiness in a church in the same breath or keystroke as championing the faith of millennials. A cursory scroll through the lexicon of millennials can be a wild mix of the discouraging and inscrutable, and trends are part of how we measure the worth of a story, tweet, or post. I'll resist the temptation to replicate the vernacular of the generation here, knowing it evolves quickly enough to make any attempt to contain it instantly laughable. Avoiding specifics, however, we can explore the broader themes.

The vocabulary of love as expressed by millennials is ever-evolving, ever more effusive, more audacious, and even silly. Much of it is, of course, hyperbolic and a way to express the inner angst of young adulthood in ever-more-theatrical terms. Our language pushes forward the options on social media modalities, which in turn pushes forward our language, all of which attempt to express the ineffable. Likes turn to loves. The drama increases—I die for this. I live for that. I love beyond love beyond love.

Through the jungle of opinions and knee-jerk reactions put forth on a daily basis, we are betrayed by our own vernacular. It may just be that millennials are calling for that which is worthy of love when all around them persists only that which can be liked. Call it suspended adolescence, call it idealism, call it whatever you like, there is something profoundly youthful and theologically beautiful about insisting on intense, deep love in a world that tells us to shed that intensity in favor of being a bit more realistic. This craving for love that is earth-shattering is a trope commonly associated with the very young, but now it seeps out in our vernacular and public expressions like never before.

It could be easy to write this off as a ridiculous trend, but I suspect there is more lurking in the depths. I suspect millennials are keenly aware that we haven't got a second to lose. Everything could change at any moment, so send us quickly the way of true love or leave us alone. We cling to this youthful type of idealism and love longer because at least some of us genuinely believe that it is the only thing that truly matters. This may be an overly generous read on the obsessive habits of status maintenance among the young, but I'm optimistic that somewhere beneath all the silliness there resides a deep well of love seeking a new form of expression.

Rather than the shallow emptiness of hyperbolic trend, what if this vernacular in fact tipped our generational hand at what lies beneath: a love ethic which echoes the great minds of justice and peace all the way back to Christ?

Love Ethic

The love ethic, a phrase popularized by Dr. Martin Luther King Jr., is rooted in the belief that love is more powerful than hate. Regardless of the vitriol being hurled your way, regardless of risk to life and limb, an unbreakable commitment to love all—including and especially thy enemies—is the central thesis. It sounds impossible and overly simplistic all at once: that immovable love should overpower hate. And yet this is at the core of what we, the church, are professing to believe. Civil rights leader Fannie Lou Hamer pulled at the same thread, famously reaching out to her captors after being jailed and beaten for seeking voting rights. Hamer refused to believe that anyone was beyond the redemption of love in Christ, and it was a belief she lived.

King, Hamer, and myriad others throughout history were committed to living with integrity that matched internal belief, professed belief, and action. A simple gut check on how often most of us in the pews live in such alignment could be revelatory. The love ethic pushes us further in the world because it prompts us to consider the exceptions to our own rules. We claim a certain level of love for all God's children, and yet who do we exclude? Which people or what categories do we imagine to be beyond salvation? And where does our action and inaction reflect those lurking beliefs beneath the surface?

What makes the love ethic so appealing and so impossible seeming is that there are no exceptions. This is at once freeing and a monumental commitment. It frees us from having to sort each other out. We are released from weighing attributes and sins for the sake of being able to neatly pin each other to a certain set of characteristics. The love ethic doesn't entail being foolish or failing to recognize that people do horrible things to one another. It just insists that, through and beyond all the horrible things we do, we persist with love.

The benefit of the love ethic is as internal as it is external. It takes a great deal of energy to hate, and it brings unimaginable peace to love, especially if love can become our default. It is a gift to embrace love and relinquish hate. However, peace doesn't negate the possibility of pain. There is often a great deal of pain and loss along the way to peace. But a *de facto* ethic of love makes it clear, both to those looking in and to ourselves, who we are and that what we say we believe defines us.

From the time I was young, my dad has consistently met my complaints about other people with a similar ethos: throw the circle of love a little wider. Always, no matter what, a little wider. It was infuriating at times when what I really wanted was for him to join me in being annoyed and petty at the perceived injustices of fifth-grade social politics, but now I see that it was an early lesson in living with the kind of impossible love ethic that Christ exhibits.

Bringing It to the Pews

One is left to wonder, then, whether authenticity of love like that is felt often in the pews. To be a bit abrupt about it: no, it isn't. The church tends to emphasize being nice or even kind and prompts us to shake hands with the stranger. We have practically perfected worship-as-performance. Our community interactions are often inauthentic and superficial, allowing us to maintain a stranglehold on our physical, emotional, and spiritual isolation. We cringe at those who overshare about their personal lives in the space of the church when, really, what could be more personal than our spiritual lives? We eschew spiritual intimacy because of how vulnerable it asks us to be, and how much we are expected to risk by telling the truth of who we are.

Make no mistake, I'm a big advocate for boundaries, both personal and professional, for the health and safety of us all. Any honest appraisal of our world makes it clear how necessary good boundaries are to creating and maintaining healthy communities. They are not fool proof, but boundaries keep us accountable and serve the end of attempting to make the church a safe place. And surely, I would contest, safe, sacred spaces and authenticity in love should not be contrary notions, but rather two aspects of a similar value. The efficacy of these boundaries depends on myriad influences. Key among these influences is the source of boundaries in a community: Were they hierarchically imposed, or did they stem from the grassroots? Are they agreed upon in consensus and do they include the voices of those most likely to be vulnerable in the community? Or are they filled with boilerplate language and then rubber-stamped into mini-law by those who already possess the greatest power in this setting?

This is no small matter of practicalities. The enforcement of boundaries of and by those in power is not the love ethic in action. Rather, to live with a sense of deeply authentic love invites the voices of the vulnerable to the center, with transparency on the part of those divesting their power for the sake of the disempowered members. In committing to policies and practices of transparency, protection of vulnerable populations, and mutual care of the community, we can practice values and protect those we claim to hold dear. Authentic love spurs people to divest power and bring the vulnerable to the table to create boundaries of consensus, rather than the superimposition of the boundaries of the powerful alone.

At the same time, we have an opportunity to dismantle the artifices that keep us spiritually remote from each other and from ourselves. The prayers of the people might actually involve the people engaging with and praying for and with one another, with time to share their actual experiences. It's true, I've seen it! The space for fellowship could be designed to prompt genuine communication instead of just polite interactions. Heck, we could encourage those with specific skills of empathy and connection to facilitate some of these moments. It is important to note that these experiences cannot be both constructed and authentic, but surely we can provide a more hospitable space for the soul than two minutes of shaking hands with anyone within reach of our seat in the pew.

I don't intend to harp on this point for the sake of critiquing the ways in which we facilitate church in one hour as it tries to meet the needs of diverse communities. I know it isn't easy. I maintain, though, that the millennial craving for authenticity and relationships which are deep and deepening is very unlikely to be satisfied in such a style. Therefore, perhaps this can help us see the ways in which it is a bit unsatisfying for all of us who are craving the kind of love Christ exhibits with his followers. A renewed emphasis on finding our roots in a love ethic would be at once monumental and a return to the most obvious aspects of who we are and what we're about in the community of Christ.

CHAPTER 10

Passion under Pressure

John 11:17–34 (NRSV)

Jesus the Resurrection and the Life

¹⁷When Jesus arrived, he found that Lazarus had already been in the tomb four days. ¹⁸Now Bethany was near Jerusalem, some two miles away, ¹⁹and many of the Jews had come to Martha and Mary to console them about their brother. ²⁰When Martha heard that Jesus was coming, she went and met him, while Mary stayed at home. ²¹Martha said to Jesus, "Lord, if you had been here, my brother would not have died. ²²But even now I know that God will give you whatever you ask of him." ²³Jesus said to her, "Your brother will rise again." ²⁴Martha said to him, "I know that he will rise again in the resurrection on the last day." ²⁵Jesus said to her, "I am the resurrection and the life. Those who believe in me, even though they die, will live, ²⁶and everyone who lives and believes in me will never die. Do you believe this?" ²⁷She said to him, "Yes, Lord, I believe that you are the Messiah, the Son of God, the one coming into the world."

Jesus Weeps

²⁸When she had said this, she went back and called her sister Mary, and told her privately, "The Teacher is here and is calling for you." ²⁹And when she heard it, she got up quickly and went to him. ³⁰Now Jesus

had not yet come to the village, but was still at the place where Martha had met him. 31 The Jews who were with her in the house, consoling her, saw Mary get up quickly and go out. They followed her because they thought that she was going to the tomb to weep there. 32 When Mary came where Jesus was and saw him, she knelt at his feet and said to him, "Lord, if you had been here, my brother would not have died." 33 When Jesus saw her weeping, and the Jews who came with her also weeping, he was greatly disturbed in spirit and deeply moved. 34 He said, "Where have you laid him?" They said to him, "Lord, come and see." 35 Jesus began to weep.

In many sermons, including ones I've preached, we zero in on Jesus in this piece of Scripture. It's got pith and power, a difficult combination for clergy to resist. Plus, it makes sense: he's central to both this and The Story, and we here receive the gift of revelation of Christ's humanity: he weeps. In just that tiny phrase, we construct a whole facet of Christ's personality: he loves his friends as dearly as any of us and, in spite of his divine insider knowledge about life in, through, and beyond death, he grieves the loss. He grieves the pain of his friends Martha and Mary as well. This is full-force feelings Jesus.

While his action is fascinating, I'm not convinced it's the most important part of the story. I think the disparity in the responses of Martha and Mary tell a much more compelling story. Given the rarity of two women with names and actual dialogue making an appearance in Scripture, I have to think the original authors agreed.

Martha goes to where Jesus is and expresses her sadness in a way that seems matter-of-fact, clear, and with a long-range vision of faith. She reassures Christ of her faith in him, and particularly emphasizes that she knows she'll see her brother again when the last day comes. Her sadness is relatable and practical. It could have been otherwise had Jesus hustled a bit more, but he didn't and so her brother is gone. Martha lives in a very practical space, with faith that consoles but doesn't request miracles.

Mary comes out with emotional guns blazing. She moves with quickness and throws herself on the ground in a moment of tearful drama. Her tone is almost accusatory and, unlike her sister, Mary does not let Christ off the hook. The subtext is plain: he should have been here. Lazarus should not be dead. Your absence has caused this heartbreaking thing to happen. Where were you when we needed you the most? Mary's passion practically explodes off the page with her hurried movements and unabashed expression of pain, anger, and anguish.

It is here that Jesus both moves and is moved. Yes, of course he weeps; a deep emotional connection with these sisters and the pain of his friend's death swim right at the surface. Perhaps he is even convicted that his absence has contributed to their pain? No way to know for sure. What is far more interesting is that here he is moved and gets going toward the tomb. Both Martha and Mary are hurt, but Martha and Christ might have continued to stay and talk in the original place of meeting had Mary not come along and passionately moved the action forward.

Passionate Protestants?

What roles do passion or conviction play in the life of the average church? I'm not talking about drama or entertainment or even that one insufferable parishioner who won't let the annual event out of their teeth though the need is no longer extant. I'm talking about from the toes to the rafters, in worship and in the world, conviction realized as expression of the call of Christ to live compassionately: to suffer with those who suffer, join in joy with those who are happy, and to weep with the brokenhearted. Where is that on any given Sunday?

In many of our mainline Protestant communities at least, passion is to be handled lightly, if at all. We wrap it up in tissue paper and put it by the good ornaments, storing it away in the worship closet which we lock so the kids won't get in there and mess it up. We mark it as precious and, as we mistakenly do too often in the church, we would rather it collect dust than risk misuse or it being broken. Like most precious aspects of faith, we mistakenly think we can possess it and control it, and passion will neither be possessed nor contained.

One very effective and efficient way we try to control passion is to put it in committee, where we often succeed in extinguishing it altogether. Committees have agendas, and usually tired participants who are eager to wrap this thing up and get home for the night. Even when we try to make committee meetings fun and inviting, the whole format remains stilted and counterintuitive. I appreciate the need for process of some sort in any group trying to make decisions as a discerning body—anarchy isn't an effective tactic in board meetings—but I do question what, if any, space is being left for those who wish to ignite passion in their community.

Even the most ardent activist among us will surely begin to soften (or simply leave in disgust) if she is meant to move through the miles of bureaucracy to have declared, about twenty years late, that her convictions are now in line with the body-wide comprehension of the Holy Spirit's movement in the world. It's exhausting. It demands a patience that the world has told us we don't have time to extend. Are we impatient for change? You'd better believe it. And thank God.

We are impatient for all the reasons previously discussed, and then some. Millennial sense of urgency is in diametric opposition to a steady-as-she-goes philosophy. We are impatient with injustice, with systems that hurt people, and with our place in holding those systems aloft. We know these systems thanks to the instantaneous and unending barrage of information out there, and we are convicted by this knowledge to do something about it. Not in a year or three or five, but now.

The early disciples didn't have much time for decision-making by committee. The earliest leaders and followers in the church were scavengers, living on the margins of a vicious empire so threatened by the smallest hint of insurrection that the response was always swift and fatal. These men and women moved evasively, putting the word before their own lives, while being persistent in the belief that the individual's survival was not as important as the truth Christ conveyed.

Luke 9:46–48 (NRSV)

True Greatness

> 46*An argument arose among them as to which one of them was the greatest.* 47*But Jesus, aware of their inner thoughts, took a little child and put it by his side,* 48*and said to them, "Whoever welcomes this child in my name welcomes me, and whoever welcomes me welcomes the one who sent me; for the least among all of you is the greatest."*

The disciples had Christ right there in their midst and they continued to be as petty and contrarian as any church committee ever. They could hardly agree on anything, and yet despite and because of them, the movement happened. The movement of Christ-following happened because it was predicated on a shared passion: to better know Christ. It is that simple and that complicated. Any movement based on following someone whose days you know on some level are numbered, necessitates haste, slicing through disagreements and skipping niceties for the sake of getting at the truth. There was no time for committee meetings.

And millennials are realizing we haven't much time for committees either. We value our freedom and capacity to chase what we are passionate about in ways that are relatively new. Much of this comes from privilege—if we were all on equal footing, then everybody would be a professional travel blogger and no one would be working graveyard shifts in a warehouse. We are not on equal footing. And yet, as we reckon with that hard reality, there is a common sensibility among many millennials that we can flex our time and talents to make many different configurations of life work in favor of pursuing passion because, to lean on a cliché, life is just way too short. So we collaborate, we celebrate each other, and we scrape together work and love and family from various aspects of life because we urgently sense the need to make every second count.

It is not a perfect comparison by any stretch because today's church must face the harsh reality that we are the new Roman Empire. We no longer exist on the margins. US Christian churches possess enormous power and privilege and this version of the church is not built to amplify non-powerful voices. Think of an average Sunday at an average church. What constrictions are in place that determine who may or may not participate? What stories are told again and again because they are easiest to amplify? Which stories get silenced because they do not have power? These decisions that feel like habits are, on some level, ongoing commitments to keep the powerful in place.

To shift to an identity of passion requires recognition of the power of the church and then an active commitment to divestment from that power. Such a shift would necessitate a willingness to examine our practices as well as our hearts, and risk the wrath of moving to new modes of, and motivations for, participation in the lives of our communities.

What I am suggesting is not a lack of power in the church but rather a lack, or overly restrained iteration, of passion. Can you not feel the deep, painful division between faith as exemplified in Christ and the weekly top-off that church has become? The distinction between life lived as a disciple and one-hour sessions before brunch? We are smothering one another in our own comfort and it's leading to a clear sense of disruption between the ways Christ called us to live and love, and how our lives actually look.

This rupture is easily traceable to a collective shift from being the oppressed and prophesying ancients to being the keepers of power. It is worthy to note that one source of such power to which the modern church can attribute her influence is false self-identification as the oppressed. When we fail to make the distinction between living well in a pluralistic world and actual honest-to-God oppression, we claim victimhood and demand pity in a way that diverts even more power in our own direction. It's a petty and dishonest move. What might hew closer to the bone of living like the church would be to recognize, engage with, and actively divest ourselves of the power we possess.

Divesting of power is at once a scary proposition and absolutely Christlike. In his act of *kenosis*—self-emptying of divinity and therefore accepting the cross—he chose humanity. Now *kenosis* does not apply in a straightforward way to our Western, US Christian experience. How could it? All of humanity surely bears the mark of the divine as children of God, but I don't see our interaction with that divinity as being removable as a sweater. That internalized divine is more eternal, and less optional. Instead, I suggest we consider our own *kenosis* as an opportunity to divest ourselves of that which dehumanizes others and, by extension dehumanizes ourselves. We needn't look very far to find the ways we dehumanize other people. We accept that our clothes are made by underpaid or unpaid laborers in inhumane conditions. We accept that our food comes to us via people who struggle to feed their own families. We're aware that our lives are in many ways propped up by those without health insurance or affordable housing. We know all these things and we're sort of fine with it as long as we can push out of our heads the ways in which we are treating our brothers and sisters as less human than ourselves. And it shouldn't be any great leap to see the ways these acts dehumanize the self as well.

This act of *kenosis* comes with no false promises. We are not offered much for emptying ourselves, and it is not that by disempowering ourselves we will become magically strong and powerful. Some treat these calls of Christ as some sort of game to figure out: if I act meek, I'll be first. If I feign weakness, I'll become much more powerful. Perhaps the call is to show *kenosis* with no prize at the bottom of the cereal box—just the reality of choosing to have less power because it is the right thing to do. It is, however, an even bigger promise at work: that to voluntarily become weak is to prioritize passion over power.

"Community organizing" is a loosely-held term, but at its core it emphasizes both process and praxis that consciously amplifies the voices, experiences, and needs of the community members themselves. Rather than maintaining external control, it conscientiously cedes power, time, and microphone/megaphone to amplify the lived realities of those on the margins. Sounds a bit Christlike to me.

The Unfairness of Life

The particular strangeness to it is that, though some may be polity wonks to be sure, very few enter the ministry because of a particular love of rules. Most of us enter for a desire to be the hands and feet of Christ in the world. I imagine most parishioners are there for the same reasons. To move, to activate, to love. We create such structure and order to keep processes clear and, theoretically, fair.

Yet the passion of millennials is rooted in a fundamental truth that disconnects us from such a possibility: we know that life is unjust and inequitable. Fair cannot exist when power is so utterly imbalanced and unchecked. The kinds of oppression that are being addressed in Safety Pin Box, the Arab Spring, Black Lives Matter, and rebellions big and small across the globe are situated in and beyond systems that are designed to ensure that oppression continues. Allow this passion, then, to prompt reflexive engagement with the ways in which the church maintains herself by keeping systems of power in her own favor as a first step toward dismantling that power for the sake of alignment with the word of God.

Understanding Privilege

Numerous illuminating books, films, plays, songs, paintings, and more have emerged in recent years with a common agenda of helping to explain what privilege is, how it moves, and the impact it has. It's a concept that seems elusive and galling to many, resistant to the idea that no matter how challenging or smooth their personal lives may be, they receive certain advantages they did not earn, based solely on class, social location, skin color, ability, and so forth. Advantages that depend in equal measure on unfair obstacles being placed in the paths of others.

The US incarcerates people, particularly people of color, at a prodigious rate, ensuring their permanent inability to participate in voting about the systems that control much of their lives. Privilege is a driving force in our nation, world, and immediate communities, and a portion of dismantling privilege is recognizing who has power, whose passion is being silenced, and how we impact one another within these systems.

We cannot begin to know the ways in which passion is confined to maintain order, a system predicated on maintaining an imbalance of power and a glut of privilege for some on the backs of many. We cannot begin to understand the energy, commitment, and lives that have been lost because our systems of power keep a few at the top and ignore the voices of the many crying out.

On a much smaller scale, privilege and power comprise the life and history of the church. Power has been collected and maintained in the hands of a few and even as changes are attempted, the monolith remains. To pretend otherwise is naïve. I hear your wariness: "My church isn't like that . . . My church is inclusive, diverse, compassionate!" Perhaps you're right, but please seek your kudos and accolades elsewhere. Until we humble ourselves and recognize that we exist as a part of a larger and frequently damaging institution, we're never going to get very far down the path Christ set. By identifying as Christians in a nation that treats Christianity as a default, a normative and central experience against which all others are compared, our lives come with some automatic privileges. Our religion won't get us extra scrutiny at airport security.

While the church may have begun under the leadership of passion, she quickly became used as a site of power. Popes, royalty, and all manner of intermingling between the two set us on a course ensuring that power was centralized among the elite and that faith and finance were permanently entwined. So far, in fact, that today the church is a paradox: a protected and powerful institution whose highest ideal is a man who opted for abject powerlessness.

So, in the face of such a paradox and even hypocrisy as this, why does this monolith stand? Because power is easy and comfortable as long as it stays invisible. The system from within a sufficiently protective coating of privilege looks like it works. The adequately housed, fed, educated and medically cared for worked hard and got what they deserved. These rules of life give us structure and meaning and a path that makes a horrific kind of sense. Horrific when you start to examine the foundations underneath and recognize the spiderweb of cracks that ensure this too shall tumble.

Passion under Pressure

We children of the new millennium are, to an extent, caught in the middle. At least some of us bought into it—the mythos of the middle class. We came of age in a world that still told us that if we followed the rules, we would have a good life, one defined as fulfilling relationships, career, family, home, retirement, etc. And we simultaneously came of age in a world that revealed how starkly untrue this is. We have seen how even those who follow every rule can still be left behind and thus are skeptical of the rules. We recognize how the rules are skewed and set based on where we were born, the color of our skin, the education levels of our parents, and the economic whims of an elite ruling class. Thanks in large part to the spread of social media and the editor-less cacophony of voices accessible everywhere and always, it has spread from a small brave group of leaders generations back to a tidal wave of consciousness. We were taught to aspire to maintain the middle class at the same time it was revealed that the US middle class is an illusion.

For a very few, this led to a myopic and even solipsistic despair, graduating college at the moment of the recession, unsure where to find meaning if not in buying a house and settling down.

For others, it signified a moment for revolution. Occupy Wall Street took to the streets in a bold, albeit chaotic, way. A wave of tech start-ups incubated the creativity of the millennials, bypassing more traditional paths of business in favor of solving problems quickly and profitably. Feminism entered a new wave, one in which we reckon with the ways we have silenced women of color. Beginning to hear the voices of women of color and recognizing the need for intersectionality is a transformative shift in the way feminism operates in the world. Equity, inclusion, and justice took roles in our discourses.

By emphasizing these principles, civil resistance is taking systemic disruption to new realms. We are learning the wisdom of prior generations that prioritizes hearing all voices, attending carefully to who has voice and power, and communicating collaboratively, with intentionality. Like so many before us, millennials are taking inspiration from the collectivity of our passion, igniting a global wave of direct action as we attempt to reshape our world.

So, in response, one could hardly expect millennials to form a committee. Why operate within a system that is dying? The church committee may be sufficient to maintain, but it hardly has the seed of revolution. If you noticed that nothing changed no matter how many times you expressed a desire for change in a politely-worded memo or at a public forum, you certainly wouldn't continue to use those means to express yourself. You'd find a new way to be heard. You'd upend the system. You'd flip some tables if you had to.

It is worth noting that the value of physically showing up is still incredibly high, even as social media enables more global, remote, and yet instantaneous presence. Social media doesn't just call us to tweet our support or post our denunciations. It calls us to give that which has a cost. Increasingly, social media calls us to show up. Now, in a mirror of the Civil Rights movement, showing up is a call to put our privilege, and therefore our bodies, on the line. If we are, because of our class, skin color, gender, political associations, etc., statistically less likely to be treated with hostility by law enforcement, then it is on the front lines that we belong. If our presence as clergy, or as a white person, or as a cisgender person can create an increase in space for those without such power to protest, then our presence is required.

Which returns us to Mary. It might just be that she was calling Christ to put his privilege on the line. Jesus, an itinerant first-century Palestinian Jew with a gift for miracles and ticking off people in power, was hardly as powerful a figure as he would become in the next few millennia. However, when it comes to privilege, Mary had even less. As a woman in a place and time that viewed women as primarily property, her voice would have been easily dismissed by anyone. Yet Christ heard her, and responded to her.

What Mary did have, however, was unmitigated passion. She demanded satisfaction.

A More Conscious Church

It would be both unfair and unwise to expect the order and practices of the church to change on a generational dime. Unfair because it insists that a new way is necessarily better, and unwise because it dismisses the value of that which came before. The church of our parents and grandparents cannot be expected to shift from session or vestry tables with our Robert's rules of order and endless cups of coffee. Wholesale abandonment of these traditions would be unlikely to produce anything more revolutionary than the traditions themselves. Those meetings could, however, begin to take into account the sense of urgency felt by so many. The institutional church could prioritize celebrating creative thinking and untested solutions to community issues. We could operate with a sense that the world's problems are our own, and not be so inhibited by our sense of slim possibilities.

Furthermore, we might consider the passion of millennials to be a virtue in assessing community needs and unstructuring ourselves. If you're not sure what your surrounding community needs the most, your average millennial will tell you: we need to go talk to the community members themselves. And, because of their giftedness at fitting into new communities, they'll likely be glad to go do it themselves. We are accustomed to carving out our own space in the conversation and tend to be aware of those voices which are silent and those people who are absent. By deconstructing committees from the same pool of participants and the same solutions to old problems, new possibilities will naturally rise. Perhaps a quality of discernment must be named, developed, and engaged across the boundaries of age and need.

While no direct comparison can effectively be made, it may be worth asking how the early disciples built a life together. It wasn't simply the loudest voice in the room that dominated all major decisions, nor could consensus have always been possible. Instead, they collaborated, fought, and labored together to become increasingly conscious of the will of God expressed through Christ. A process of the slow revelation of the power of empire throughout the world is consciousness-raising, and the church could use some more of it.

CHAPTER 11

Can't Buy This Love: Offering and Millennial Faith

Matthew 9:9–13 (NRSV)

9As Jesus was walking along, he saw a man called Matthew sitting at the tax booth; and he said to him, "Follow me." And he got up and followed him.

10And as he sat at dinner in the house, many tax collectors and sinners came and were sitting with him and his disciples. 11When the Pharisees saw this, they said to his disciples, "Why does your teacher eat with tax collectors and sinners?" 12But when he heard this, he said, "Those who are well have no need of a physician, but those who are sick. 13Go and learn what this means, 'I desire mercy, not sacrifice.' For I have come to call not the righteous but sinners."

This is one of my favorite iterations of Christ: practicing the naming of things, recognizing that he couldn't focus all his energy on those who were already doing okay, but rather that there were those on the margins who needed him more. He sees who he sees and pursues who he pursues and doesn't waste a lot of time trying to make that make sense to those around him. Somewhere in the mix of genuinely altruistic evangelism—literally bearing the good news to others—and the night-sweat-inducing terror of churches losing members and money, the institutional church trend is toward not rocking the boat. It's the fallacious notion that church can and should be all things to all people (as should pastors for that matter, but that's another book for another day). It's hard to picture any pastor at all saying with such absolute confidence to her parishioners: *actually, I'm not here for you, I'm here for them.* We don't do that. We try to corral and maintain our membership as it looks, only adding, never decreasing.

The church has many less-than-desirable habits, but perhaps among the very worst is attendance shaming. "Oh it's so good to see you—we were wondering what happened to you!" "We haven't seen you in weeks!" And, my personal favorite, "Is this your first time here?" "No . . . I've been coming here for years." (Pro-tip: always lead with "it's so good to see you!" This is infinitely safer.)

I've gone to all-out tiny war to get rid of "friendship pads." I've dealt in backroom bargains with the administrative staff to stop the practice of printing the previous weeks' attendance in the bulletin. And I've (lovingly) shoved church leaders toward considering ways of telling our story beyond taking attendance and counting dollars. I've done this not because friendship pads and attendance-keeping don't yield some valuable information, but because they miss the point of church and are, frankly, *screaming* the insecurities of the church right out loud.

Pastors fall into this trap as much as anyone and frequently more so since their immediate financial livelihood is tied to the church's survival. We stress about budgets and fundraising efforts and stewardship campaigns. We do our best to equally value all our parishioners' opinions regardless of their pledge amount, but it is hard to ignore the wishes of your boss, which happens when we forget that our only boss is God.

The insecurity seeps into the pews though, no doubt about it. It's the petitioning for volunteers that turns into a harangue, and the eighteenth reminder of the upcoming fall carnival fundraiser. It's the letters beseeching contributions to close the budget shortfall and banking on minimal snow on Christmas Eve so the donations look as-anticipated.

And insecurity isn't a good look on anyone, let alone the church. It's certainly not bad to be passionate, but it is irritating to have passion only show up as a white-knuckled and fearful grip on self-preservation. Here, insecurity gives an undue amount of power to the whims of the world. People can sense this and millennials seem particularly put off by it. Given that we exist in an increasingly secular world, with myriad other options of what to do with our time, if you don't believe in what you're doing, why should we?

If we are convinced that the church will fold up shop beyond some imaginary line of attendance or giving, then we are lost in the motivation of sustaining our own version of the world. The message of God will be drowned out by our sense of self-preservation. We should not pretend that we don't care about survival because that would be dishonest. Of course, we care if this institution into which we have put life and labor and love survives, but perhaps we could raise the standard a bit on how we understand the survival of the church beyond our corner of the world.

Survival, in the context of the church, has to be about the sustenance of God's love through the acts of people. God's got the God's love part covered. God is our one endlessly renewable resource. What remains is that which is our responsibility: living out that love through compassion, dedication, and care. If our only real metric of the success and survival of a church had to do with how fully they lived the word of God in compassionate action, we would have a very different barometer for measuring survival.

The church of Jesus Christ does not live or die on what we do each Sunday. Or how many people attended our last Christmas Eve service. It relies on something much bigger and stronger than that, and the ways we present what we're about should live and die on that truth, not the other way around.

A hard piece of that truth is that Christ did not build his church on a foundation of cruise-ship-directing as ministry. Too often, church becomes about entertaining people, hooking in the sought-after demographics (as if there were demographics of humanity that shouldn't be sought after by the church), and keeping people happy. The original intent of the church was never about maintaining a low level of contentment and keeping the weekly donations rolling in through activities that delight and placate. If Christ had wanted that sort of thing, I imagine he would have left the Sadducees and Pharisees to their own devices.

Christ makes it very clear that he came for this, not that, and for them, not these. His work is intentional, focused, and unconventional. All of this flies in the face of a theological interpretation of Jesus who loves us all as little children, the belief that we are here only to receive the love of God rather than do the work of God. Christ certainly has much to teach every single one of us, but he came for some direct purposes. We would do well to not mask those in feel-good-ery.

CAN'T BUY THIS LOVE: OFFERING AND MILLENNIAL FAITH

Keeping the original expressed purposes of Christ in a direct line of sight and pursuing them wholeheartedly is the single clearest way out of the offering minefield that this particular millennial can envision.

Offering

Plenty of organizations are happy to tell you about improving the mechanics of giving in a new era, and much of the advice is sound: offer online giving options; have a credit card-reading square at the ready for fundraisers because almost nobody carries cash or a checkbook; recognize the premium value placed on time when you are asking young people to give of themselves to fundraising efforts; and bear in mind that creativity will out-value longevity for most of us.

Once you've got the mechanics figured out, it's time to better know a millennial and attempt to see a fuller picture of what you're asking and from whom. While I'd like you to find a millennial of your own and inquire about their life experiences, we can start with James.

James is twenty-four and relatively new to your city. He was raised Lutheran and makes it a practice to find a Lutheran church when he moves to a new town, which is how he ended up at your church on Sunday. James has just finished his master's degree in communication having been (rightly) convinced that in today's job market, a B.A. in English has about the earning power of a high school diploma fifteen years ago. James has $22,000 in student loans, which he's paying off at about $300 a month. His monthly rent on a one-bedroom in an okay-ish neighborhood is $1,550. All of his other expenses (utilities, food, cell phone, gas, and car maintenance, etc.) come to about $1,800 a month. He works as a junior editor for a growing news website and does both contract grant-writing and data entry on the side, netting an annual income of $45,000. He and his long-time partner are trying to save up for a wedding and his family wants him to visit home several states away far more often than he does. He's netting about $200 a month for savings or a social life. Now, after he's attended your church community for a few months, you ask him to make an annual pledge that will quantify his monthly giving in dollars and cents. This is the collision of two totally different worlds.

Bearing in mind that James is deeply average, ask yourself: How does tithing work when you work three part-time jobs just to get by? How does investing in the church make it onto the radars of students with tens and even hundreds of thousands of dollars of student debt, a great many of whom graduated college just in time for the largest economic depression in living memory for most Americans? This isn't to make excuses for millennials and their spending habits, but to recognize the skyrocketing costs and painful realities of student loans as they were taken out to achieve what has become a ground-floor necessity in the professional world millennials are entering.

Millennials' highest level of indebtedness is their student loans, according to Gallup. Those millennials with student loans end up paying about 36 percent of their annual income to pay down those loans. Combined with other forms of consumer debt, millennials with student loans are paying about 57 percent of their annual income toward their debts. This isn't counting things like rent, food, or insurance ("Millennials: the Job-Hopping Generation," Gallup, May 12, 2016). These figures give us a glimpse into the ways the twenty-something's experience looks vastly different than the twenty-something's experiences of generations before, and bear enormous influence on the investment decisions millennials will make.

Not that there is an overabundance of understanding or support coming from other generations on this topic. The accusations are hilarious: that we spend too much on our brunches and are therefore collectively demolishing industries from diamonds to home-buying. The truth is closer to this: that home ownership will remain a distant dream for many, many millennials. And, by and large, we're okay with it.

Part of this okayness is survival: we know despair won't get us anywhere and, as previously mentioned, we figured out a while back that our futures would little resemble our parents' pasts. We are okay with needing to forge a new path, and to rely on our creativity and sense of enterprise over previously reliable ways of living. Part of the okayness is newfound expressions of how utterly not okay our systems of finance are in this country: a dawning revelation of the sheer gob-smacking, mind-boggling levels of corruption in our financial systems.

We are, indeed, the generation of Occupy Wall Street (OWS) and other grassroots movements toward the abolition of financial institutions. OWS was a unique animal even among contemporary peers in protest. A deliberately leaderless movement, it suffered under the misapprehensions of those it was most intent to persuade, leading to false assumptions about the laziness and entitlement of these people making a mess in Zucotti Park.

Can't Buy This Love: Offering and Millennial Faith

Underneath the cross-talk and messaging issues, OWS drew out a generational collective voicing opposition against giants with near omnipotent control over the American experience. You've got to admire the pluck. Facing those who would determine who gets a student loan and their rates of payback, who determine who qualifies for a home loan and who does not, who wield unimaginable power, these kids in tents fought back.

They fought against the reality that the US functions, as does any empire, on the backs of the poor, and keeping a distinction between classes is essential to maintaining order as it looks. OWS stood in opposition to this idea, insisting that they didn't come for the poor: they were here for the hearts and minds of Wall Street. Sounds a bit familiar, really.

There is a groundswell of support for candidates advocating a more socialist agenda and it should surprise exactly no one that the largest pool of support for Bernie Sanders came from millennials, concerned for the mounting debt, lack of health care, and lack of equity in education, safety, or criminal justice reform.

The Occupy movement was a strange confluence of events, and debating its relative success or failure as a movement is a topic for another text. It certainly was not an ostensibly religious movement, though they were coming for the modern-day tax collectors. It was a movement about upsetting the dynamics of empire that kept the powerful gaining ever-more power, while the powerless increasingly diminished.

OWS operated in a similar fashion to the early church by disrupting norms. OWS used intentionally inclusive communication, expressions of stance without signed authorship, for the sake of prioritizing principles as opposed to people, and remained open to the ways their movement could shift based on the lived needs of the community. Likewise, Paul's letters help solidify our understanding that even the early churches included a lot of chaos, at least from the outside looking in. Though expressed with love, Paul was quick to squash any attempts to glorify individuals over the central point of Christ's message. The early apostles worked hard to dismantle attempts to codify rules over righteousness. Or, put another way, the Way and the Word came first.

Such movements as OWS also serve to draw out the need for a fresh definition of a word at the heart of so much boomer-based philosophy on the nature of giving at church: legacy.

Legacy

Leaving a legacy is common parlance in the church world. We want to offer something beautiful and/or useful to mark that We Stood Here, offering up glory to God and a signpost by which our progeny might remember us. This is predicated on the idea that the institutional church is a place of physical permanence, where we can count on our stained-glass window being around for generations to come, despite all evidence to the contrary. What becomes of this sort of legacy, then, if and when the institution crumbles?

Too much of our sense of stewardship is wrapped up in this concept of legacy, and we've got to become cognizant of the fact that legacy means something completely different to millennials. A legacy of donating a new rose window in the name of great-aunt Jane is a lovely and moving gesture—and, less dramatically than questioning what should happen if the church should crumble, one that rests on the assumption that one's church will remain one's church forever.

Can we make legacy portable? How? Perhaps by incarnating those words of Christ: "I desire mercy, not sacrifice" (Matt 9:13, referencing Hos 6:6).

Mission as Legacy

To begin this radical shift in financial philosophy, a church must begin by interrogating their sense of giving. A more refined concept than simply rewriting our annual report with enough anecdotes and charming photos and getting the most endearing elders to do the big stewardship ask, we must ask ourselves why anyone, let alone cash-strapped millennials, should give to this work.

Does mercy fit into your church's conception of giving? How about grace? How about justice? If you can't articulate how your philosophy of each informs the way you talk about stewardship to the church, don't expect a ton of investment from the millennial crowd. If it sounds foreign or even silly to talk about mercy in the context of building a church budget, perhaps that is sufficiently illuminating my point. How have we let the identity of the church slide so far from her original intended purposes?

When I speak of working with concepts of mercy, grace, and justice in the church's financial plans, I do not only mean the outputs: that we give to these organizations that practice those principles on our behalf. I mean the actual interior working and life of the church herself. Who or what are we stewarding through the life of our very congregation? How are we behaving as just, merciful, gracious people to one another, as well as to those who live near or enter the building in which we worship, as well as the rest of the world?

Rather, reach beyond the maintenance of the status quo and consider inviting participation (financial and otherwise—and the otherwise matters a great deal here) into the mission of the church as the common legacy in which all play a part. Let our communal identity become our shared legacy of mission.

It is so ludicrously easy to give to organizations we care about. With a few swipes on the phone, we can give instantly to disaster relief organizations we trust in real time as the disaster continues to unfold. Methods by which we can discern the transparency and credibility of an organization are also at our fingertips. There is an increasingly shared sense that our giving needs to honor the dignity of those to whom we give and that those organizations running intermediary be held to a higher-than-ever standard of authenticity about their work. It has become common among millennials to call organizations—particularly philanthropic ones—to account for their practices. There is widespread circulation of data on Facebook or Twitter regarding the salaries of CEOs of various charities or the percentage of donations that go to cover salaries as opposed to direct service. All this information can help would-be donors make choices that align with their sense of integrity. Churches would do well to share a similar style of transparency, not buried in an annual report, but with authenticity and joy that their requests for stewardship align so well with their lived reality.

Most of those who are philanthropically inclined are already giving to the organizations that matter most to us, often as a manifestation of our faith. Does your church's self-concept have the capacity to include these gifts when counting the impact you have on the world?

Consider it this way: James hears a sermon about ethnic cleansing in Myanmar from his pastor. Perhaps a more in-depth study of the region comes about in adult ed. He is moved, compelled unto action, convicted in the way that we hope people who come to church will be convicted.

Then James's own research leads him to a grassroots organization that does the exact work he finds most compelling as a manifestation of his conviction that, indeed, Christ would want us to interrupt genocide. James starts giving $50 a month directly to that group.

Now, is James giving to the work of the church? I would argue yes, absolutely. This small move toward a more expansive and inclusive view of giving could instigate an avalanche of change in a church's self-identification. Connecting the web of giving and living, volunteer hours, and work done beyond the walls of the church could highlight a broader appreciation of giving and bond parishioners more concretely in relationship and identity of discipleship.

To the point of valuing gifts "otherwise" than financial, as mentioned before: let us not give lip service to time and talents. Either value them equally to financial contributions or be honest about not valuing them at all.

I hear you, friends. "That's all very nice as an idea but who is going to pay to keep the lights on and cover the sexton's salary?" Reasonable concerns. Reasonable, at least, in an unreasonable world that insists we cling on to the notion that there is just this one way to do and be church. Might I suggest another page from the millennial handbook? Our aforementioned balancing act of debt, multiple jobs, mobility, and so forth has equipped us with the gifts of flexibility, creativity, and scrappiness. And Lord knows the church could use some scrappiness.

Scrappiness: Where Mercy Meets Sacrifice

When Christ recalls the prophet Hosea and challenges listeners to understand what it means to say "I desire mercy, not sacrifice," he is calling us out to remember that law without love behind it is a pretty empty gesture. Sacrifice which focuses only on the self is sacrifice without mercy. This isn't a declaration that sacrifice isn't valuable, just that it isn't the most valuable thing. Instead, mercy is the worthier part.

Therefore, it just might be that millennials' offerings of scrappiness could facilitate a reimagining of church structure and praxis that allows us to dismantle the sacrificial ways we consider our finances in favor of placing mercy front and center. What if every single decision our leadership boards and bodies had to make—from switching to fair-trade coffee to our public positions on community issues—was first required to pass the litmus test of whether what we are doing is merciful?

CHAPTER 12

The Revolution Will Be Tweeted

Matthew 3 (NRSV)

The Proclamation of John the Baptist

In those days John the Baptist appeared in the wilderness of Judea, proclaiming, 2 "Repent, for the kingdom of heaven has come near." 3 This is the one of whom the prophet Isaiah spoke when he said,

"The voice of one crying out in the wilderness:
'Prepare the way of the Lord,
make his paths straight.'"

4 Now John wore clothing of camel's hair with a leather belt around his waist, and his food was locusts and wild honey. 5 Then the people of Jerusalem and all Judea were going out to him, and all the region along the Jordan, 6 and they were baptized by him in the river Jordan, confessing their sins.

7 But when he saw many Pharisees and Sadducees coming for baptism, he said to them, "You brood of vipers! Who warned you to flee from the wrath to come? 8 Bear fruit worthy of repentance. 9 Do not presume to say to yourselves, 'We have Abraham as our ancestor'; for I tell you, God is able from these stones to raise up children to Abraham. 10 Even now the ax is lying at the root of the trees; every tree therefore that does not bear good fruit is cut down and thrown into the fire.

> ¹¹*"I baptize you with water for repentance, but one who is more powerful than I is coming after me; I am not worthy to carry his sandals. He will baptize you with the Holy Spirit and fire.* ¹²*His winnowing fork is in his hand, and he will clear his threshing floor and will gather his wheat into the granary; but the chaff he will burn with unquenchable fire."*

John the Baptist points the way. The Neville Longbottom to Jesus's Harry Potter, John the Baptist is too often treated like a side character when in truth he's vital to the story. His birth foretold, his death overloaded with meaning, John spent his days attempting to ready the world for one like Christ.

My hunch is this: that while both institutional church and millennial Christians accept Christ as savior, the boomer belief is a focus on the maintenance of Christ's life and work, while the millennial belief is that the work is happening. What I mean is this: we can focus our energy on memorializing, remembering, and retelling the stories of Christ as the treasures that they are. We can inspire a sense of good will and some satisfaction that we follow a guy who did things right. We can remember the way he healed the sick, the tormented, and the blind, and live in awe of those miracles. That is definitely an option, and, as Scripture is so central to our worship and praxis, it's a natural default.

Or we can approach Scripture in a much more John-the-Baptist fashion. He couldn't possibly have known what was really coming, but he trusted his prophetic and locust-filled gut enough to move in a direction that led people into the glorious unknown. We can, therefore, approach Scripture as more of a mystery still unfolding, and one which allows for a sense of possibility at its very heart. Both the work of creation and the work of sustenance matter in Scripture and might matter in life just as much.

John's work mattered and John knew it. He spread his prophecy because he couldn't do otherwise. He was deferential to Christ because he knew his work was all about Christ, preparing the path, attempting to get the people ready. But he didn't do this simply by sitting and waiting. He did it by doing the work, speaking to whomever would listen, placing his body and mind on the line for this work of preparation.

John's work included irritating people, a common path for prophets to walk. Prophecy involves saying the unpopular thing in an unpopular way, eschewing easy alliances in favor of a life lived with full integrity. John and all the prophets modeled the high risks involved in speaking clear observations of the world as it is and prophesying about what may come to pass given a current trajectory. This hasn't gotten a whole lot more popular in the ensuing centuries, as those in power never really enjoy hearing that their destruction may be imminent. Doesn't make it any less true, though.

Let's pause a moment to consider what it means to have integrity: to be, literally, integrated. To be more than just whole, but a whole that is aligned and operates under a consistency of beliefs and practices that are congruent all down the line. All the pieces work in concert. John's work calls us to this kind of life as a means of readying ourselves for Christ.

A Season of Revolutions

I sit to write this chapter the day after Charlottesville, Virginia happened. In the dark days when the racism, misogyny, and hate that have so long comprised the underbelly of the US are being laid bare, a group of open and proud white supremacists marched with (tiki) torches on the town of Charlottesville. Their presence and chanting to "unite the right" was ostensibly to express anger about the removal of a statue of Robert E. Lee, and there was a clear degree of horrifying pride in their message. These people—predominantly young, predominately male, exclusively white—marched with their faces bare and angry. They didn't crave anonymity, they craved visibility. They marched for, presumably, the same reason many of us march for other causes: to protest and to feel reassured that there are more of us than there are of you. Marching marks our existence and makes visible that which was hidden. When this takes the form of the march on Selma, it's a powerful and moving lived example of the bravery of oppressed people—and let us be mindful to not dissolve into sentimentalizing the danger, violence, and loss experienced by those who marched. Theirs was an act of bravery. When it's a bunch of white supremacist trolls come out from their basements to feign strength through intimidation, it is pathetic.

Regardless of whether this proves to be one more in an unending stream of battles between the key ideological differences of the US (namely: Is white supremacy acceptable to us or not? And there is only one correct answer—that it is not.) or not, or a key turning point, the remarkable speed of data shared and opinions voiced was astonishing.

It took less than a day for doxxing, a form of vigilante internet justice and a frequent tactic of internet trolls, to become a tool of the counter-protestors. By using the vast data we willingly share about ourselves to publicize the name, photo, occupation, and history of any person photographed with the white supremacists, counter-protestors worked to circulate the images broadly. Widespread attempts were made to get these men, so eager to show their faces as poster boys for hate, publicly humiliated, fired from jobs, etc., And in at least a few cases, it seems to have been an effective tactic, with individuals being publicly denounced by their families and friends and let go from their places of employment.

The tactic is swift and can be enormously cruel. It falls among the techniques of groups like Antifa, seeking to destabilize the platforms of fascist hate groups, as well as among the tactics of hate groups themselves. It's a way to apply social pressure writ large. Right or wrong, it signifies a new world in which the movement of social justice moves faster than ever before.

My personal branch of the social media universe is intentionally small, and wildly disproportionately populated by liberals, progressives, and clergy-people, so it is unsurprising that the responses filling my feed yesterday contained numerous calls for preachers to throw out their prepared sermons and speak the truth to power, that white supremacy find no safe quarter in the house of God.

The Baptism of Jesus

> 13 *Then Jesus came from Galilee to John at the Jordan, to be baptized by him.* 14*John would have prevented him, saying, "I need to be baptized by you, and do you come to me?"* 15 *But Jesus answered him, "Let it be so now; for it is proper for us in this way to fulfill all righteousness." Then he consented.* 16*And when Jesus had been baptized, just as he came up from the water, suddenly the heavens were opened to him and he saw the Spirit of God descending like a dove and alighting on him.* 17*And a voice from heaven said, "This is my Son, the Beloved, with whom I am well pleased."*

I once served communion in a community that welcomed everyone forward, regardless of age or membership or anything else. One tiny member of that community moved toward the front of the line to receive the elements and looked warily from the plate of tiny pieces of bread to me, and then to the loaf of bread that had been broken recently. "Do you want some of this instead?" I asked, offering the loaf of bread in his direction, eye-checking his mother to make sure it was alright. With a grin, he grabbed the loaf of bread from my hands and walked back to his seat, happily munching away on his new snack. I imagine God was well pleased with that little one. Let there always be such a sense of abundance in the house of God.

I don't imagine that anyone bothering to read this far in a book like this would voice any opposition to my earlier statement that white supremacy is anathema to the church. Perhaps you're even a bit insulted by the suggestion. "There are no klanspeople here!" While that's hopefully true, the inculcation of white supremacy into every facet of US life requires some painful, intentional self-exploration and revelation for participants in mostly or completely white communities of faith.

I'd like to challenge the church to abolish the politics of respectability, the most common way racism shows up in our pews. The phrase "politics of respectability" refers to a way by which we socially police each other. It is on the crummy and crumbling foundation of respectability that we convince ourselves of lies big and small: that there is a right way to dress, sing, speak, and be, particularly in church, and anyone who wants in is most welcome as long as they fit these standards of presentation and behavior. Respectability politics insists, subtly, that the poor just don't work hard enough, that people of color should attempt to look or sound white to be recognized as worthy, and that everybody needs to speak English to be an American. It is, in a word, nonsense.

The politics of respectability are the control mechanism that keeps white supremacy present and notably silent in our pulpits and pews. It keeps us more worried about what the girls wear on the mission trip than whether the boys are being taught to lead a charge against rape culture. Respectability emphasizes modesty, politeness, and an allegiance to a set of social codes meaning that many, many people are kept out and nothing can ever change in the life of the church. It's the exact opposite of the way millennials are pushing for social change.

Social Movements in Real Time

The momentum of social movements in the past decade or two must necessarily give homage to new technology-organizing mechanisms. The Arab Spring caught on camera and tweeted a movement to life. Though a slightly dated example, the occurrence of the Arab Spring in nations with state-controlled media is breathtaking. Through a series of illicit internet connections and anonymously held accounts, the moment-to-moment events happening in Tahrir Square and elsewhere could be published to the world, effectively countering the messages of state-controlled media. By enabling outsiders to be in-the-moment with the protestors, the Arab Spring garnered global attention and widespread support that encouraged them. Though far away, the protesters were not alone.

Black Lives Matter has likewise proven the power of real-time footage. Videos of men and women of color encountering police violence sheds light on intimate yet universal and profoundly valid fears. While heartbreaking beyond measure, the cell phone footage of police brutality and murders of persons of color, jumping from news feed to news feed, has shaped the discourse by clarifying this reality for those without direct experience of it. A white person cannot understand what it means to experience law enforcement as a person of color experiences it, and building understanding through the lived experiences others choose to share can help illuminate how little is understood. While this road to understanding is far from smooth or easy, it is no longer a road we can ignore or pretend we don't see as necessary to walk.

Millennials bring a particular savvy about the use of such technology, including the need for caution and resistance to the machinery of technology itself. Facebook, for example, is not without profit or agenda, and resistance leaders know this too well from the experience of having their posts removed or their pages dismantled. Corporate and political agendas, combined with an imperfect system of reporting (that allows any user to report any other for perceived infractions), allow for the fact that sometimes the system of dissemination reinforces the system of oppression. Operating within these modalities requires a level of conscientiousness, as well as persistence and creativity.

Similar habits show up in the church by her silence: we don't tend to engage with movements until they've passed us by, until we have the security of numbers and amendments, until it has become respectable and even expected rather than prophetic. The Civil Rights movement, almost universally praised today, was treated with open hostility and derision by many in its moment. I watched my own denomination debate the full inclusion of the LGBTQIA community decades after large swaths of the world had figured out that such inclusion just makes sense for a system of faith that recognizes the inherent worth of all people. This argument went on for years, up and down through our systems of polity and governance, hurting a great many people along the way. In the end, we came down on the side of full inclusion, lost a chunk of our community to their own interpretation of Scripture, and came out woefully behind our peers. I'm grateful for where we landed, but ashamed it took us that long to get there.

Millennials might take a cue from John on this one. To follow Christ is to lead people on a new and strange path, and to risk being seen as impolite, disrespectful, and even a bit out of touch with life. Be willfully idealistic.

These views were not held strictly by millennials to be sure, but it is using the tools of the millennium to call one another to action that inspires a new possibility.

I imagine the church would become a much more complicated place if we considered that Christ doesn't much agree with the idea of some people deserving grace and mercy while others don't because they wore the wrong outfit or didn't pick up on the fact that they were making people uncomfortable. In fact, I think Christ rather liked making people uncomfortable. He was darn good at it. And so too must we be.

Conclusion

In the end, millennials are exactly like every generation before us. That might seem like a slightly ludicrous claim after spending the last dozen chapters trying to persuade you that there are unique and wonderful things about the millennial generation. I do believe there are great, glorious things about this generation that the church and US society at large would do well to consider and appreciate. I also believe that, in the end, we are all more alike than different, and this generation is just the same. We are optimistic and insecure, overconfident and feeling woefully behind. We hold a multiplicity of beliefs and grip our convictions for dear life until we are invited and able to see beyond them.

But we are here and we are not attempting to ruin anything except that which needs to be changed. Make no mistake, that which needs to change will change with or without us. Institutions have a way of doing that to themselves when it becomes necessary. As I've tried to reassure many individuals and churches: the work of Jesus Christ does not live or die on the decisions any of us make. It will not disappear with any one denomination's rise or fall. It certainly will not disappear due to changes made by any one generation. Let's breathe easy and maintain some faith that Christ is way bigger than any of us and our people-sized problems.

Fear not: the church changes shape every few centuries and we're past due. See us then as harbingers of potentially meaningful change, bearing a host of skills, passion, and perhaps even a prophetic word or two. Know we may turn things on their head and that might be exactly what the church needs most of all.

Some suggestions for reading this book as a church community: Do what you can to avoid reading it in generational isolation. I would be baffled if you agreed with everything included in these pages, regardless of your age or experience. Since I can't be there to argue in love face to face, please do your best to find a diversity of perspectives with which to share and discuss this text. And then do what we've gotten quite bad at doing in the church: genuinely engage each other. Don't be shy about interrogating ideas: mine, your own, each others'.

Discussion Questions

1) Where do you see millennials fitting into the life of your church? How about God's church?

2) What aspects of the book do you disagree with and why? Beneath this, consider how disagreement manifests in the life of your church. What does it look like? Who speaks and who is silent? Why?

3) Who or what is out of bounds for your faith community? Think of those who came and left, and those who have never come at all. Tell the stories and then ask yourselves out loud why this is the case.

4) What is the one big fear that motivates decisions in your community? What is the one big hope that does the same? Which of these two more clearly shapes the identity of your church?

5) What do you find convicting in this book?

6) What comes next?

www.ingramcontent.com/pod-product-compliance
Lightning Source LLC
Chambersburg PA
CBHW020855160426
43192CB00007B/941